CHARLES MACKAY'S

EXTRAORDINARY POPULAR DELUSIONS AND THE MADNESS OF CROWDS

CHARLES MACKAY'S

EXTRAORDINARY POPULAR DELUSIONS AND THE MADNESS OF CROWDS

A MODERN-DAY INTERPRETATION
OF A FINANCE CLASSIC
BY TIM PHILLIPS

Copyright © Infinite Ideas Limited, 2009

The right of Tim Phillips to be identified as the author of this book has been asserted in accordance with the Copyright, Designs and Patents Act 1988.

First published in 2009 by
Infinite Ideas Limited
36 St Giles
Oxford
OX1 3LD
United Kingdom
www.infideas.com

A CIP catalogue record for this book is available from the British Library

ISBN 978–1–905940–91–2

Brand and product names are trademarks or registered trademarks of their respective owners.

Designed and typeset by Cylinder

Cover image reproduction: Special Collections Library Wageningen UR, speccoll.library@wur.nl

Printed in India

BRILLIANT IDEAS

INTRODUCTION

Extraordinary Popular Delusions and the Madness of Crowds **isn't a short book. As its title suggests, Charles Mackay didn't favour three words where he thought eight would do the job.**

It's definitely a Victorian book, but it's a modern one too. As we will see, the popular delusions that he ridicules persist to this day – we just give them different names. Each time they recur through history, we are surprised and mortified that we were swept up in Ponzi schemes, conned by smooth hucksters, victims of mass hysteria, controlled by demagogues and seduced by investments that simply cannot lose.

We're living a global sitcom, one in which no one learns anything from episode to episode, and we make the same mistakes over and over again – while convincing ourselves that this time we're right, and it's different. Mackay's catalogue of our own craziness, spanning about a millennium, was the first book to demonstrate what scientists now know: when we act in groups we're often not very smart.

The best-known bits of the book are about business, and about what we now call economic 'bubbles' where speculation increases a price out of all reason – before it crashes. Mackay's history of the Mississippi Scheme, the South Sea Bubble and the 'Tulipomania' are commerce retold as farce.

Other parts of the book deal with charlatans and con men: the fortune tellers and magnetisers, for example, who convince us they've got a secret talent to heal or reveal the future, and then hand us the bill. As you will see, they're still with us today, and they are possibly more successful than ever.

The sections on the witch mania and the Crusades show us that when we look for enemies, whether those enemies exist or not, we're prepared to condemn or even kill thousands of innocent people on the flimsiest of pretexts.

And the weird patterns of fashion and strange behaviour, popular beliefs and follies that we all share without thinking about it – admiring thieves, believing in ghosts – undermine our claims to be rational.

Mackay was incredibly well-read and thorough, so almost all of the hard-to-believe stories stand up to scrutiny 150 years later. Indeed, much of the last 150 years has been a demonstration that we can be even madder than Mackay thought. The incredible histories, some of which have almost been lost to us, show how irrational and dangerous groups of people have always been. But this is not a history book. Anyone in Europe or the US who has opened a newspaper recently will agree with Mackay that 'sober nations have all at once become desperate gamblers'. When we laugh at the stupidity of the people in his book, we're laughing at ourselves.

Your recovery starts here.

1 TOO MANY REPEATS

In his introduction to the 1852 edition of *Extraordinary Popular Delusions*, Mackay points out that 'whole communities suddenly fix their minds upon one object, and go mad with its pursuit'. Sounds familiar? The whole book could have been written yesterday.

DEFINING IDEA...

Those who cannot remember the past, are condemned to repeat it.

~ GEORGE SANTAYANA

'Men, it has been well said, think in herds; it will be seen that they go mad in herds, while they only recover their senses slowly, and one by one,' Mackay says. He goes on, '...popular delusions began so early, spread so widely, and have lasted so long, that instead of two or three volumes, fifty would scarcely suffice to detail their history'.

Inside those two statements are the essence of why he wrote his book – and why I am writing this. To Mackay first: his working theory was that mass delusions carry everyone along with them, causing all kinds of trouble: the ruin of people who have spent their lives carefully saving, to then throw it all in on a speculation; the vilification of an innocent scapegoat; the waste of time and money on some grand project that is unreachable or unworkable. We think the wrong thing not because we simply reached the wrong conclusion (which he, and most people, would consider pardonable) but often because the others around us are thinking it too.

But the retreat from madness is a far slower and more painful process, initiated by one or two who have the bravery and the strength of intellect not to run with the crowd for the sake of it. They often achieve the most profit, or take the smallest loss, for their lonely integrity. Gradually others follow. They see the example of the pioneers, ask 'what was I thinking?' and detach themselves from the crowd.

Much later, the crowd, like a flock of starlings, may reconsider and set off in a new direction too. They might ask, 'what was I thinking?', but it's an empty question. They weren't thinking as individuals then and they are not now; all they have done is to follow a new crowd. In a financial panic, they are the ones who get ruined.

If this was purely of historical interest, then so would the book be. But, as we will see, there are thousands of examples of exactly the same behaviour that Mackay deplored back then which are still around today. We know about the South Sea Bubble, but Mackay's contemporaries still created the Railway Mania and we fell for the dot-com boom. We regret the persecution of witches, but our grandparents lived through the imprisonment of communists, and today mobs have Asian holidaymakers thrown off commercial flights because they were talking in a foreign language, and so must be terrorists.

We don't need fifty books; we live the same book over and over, with a different cast list. Delusions are as popular as ever.

HERE'S AN IDEA FOR YOU...

At work, create the official position of Devil's Advocate for any project. That person has the role of questioning your decisions and assumptions, to make sure your herd doesn't go mad.

2 TOO GOOD TO BE TRUE

'How easily the masses have been led astray,' laments Mackay, in the introduction to the 1841 edition of his book. We still think we can get something for nothing today.

When banks, shops, police and our parents warn us against fraud, it's not unusual for them to tell us 'if something looks too good to be true, it usually is'. As you chuckle at the stupidity of eighteenth-century speculators, remember that we're no smarter.

DEFINING IDEA...
Rather fail with honour than succeed by fraud.
~ SOPHOCLES

Someone passed an email to me recently: 'Compliments of the day to you. Following the Global Economic Direct Investment Scheme. I want to do business for the benefit of the both of us to boost economic ties and build on the changing business climate in your country ... Let me introduce myself, As the British foreign secretary, I got your contact from the internet security directory affiliated to my office and I want to invest £40,000,000 (forty million) british pounds sterling in your reputable company...'

Yes, it's a variation on the classic Nigerian advance fee fraud (also known as 419 fraud, after the Nigerian law that it breaks). This one was more entertaining than most, as it claimed to come from David Miliband MP.

Modern 419 scams work like this: you will get an email from someone you've never heard of. It promises you vast wealth if you help in some way – often by supplying your bank details so that a distressed foreign royal or businessperson can park their money in your account (the idea of using the Foreign Secretary's name is rather creative). There are two outcomes: either someone cleans out your account using the information you have kindly donated, or the plot thickens – usually by you receiving a counterfeit cheque, paying it into your account, and making a payment to them in return. Either way, you will never see your millions.

The 419 frauds started as faxes and telexes in the 1980s but email has enabled swindlers all over the world, though West Africa now has a flourishing business in 419 fraud. This is now estimated by Insa Nolte, a lecturer in African culture at the University of Birmingham, to be one of Nigeria's most important export industries.

The fraudsters have been remarkably successful. It's tough to work out exactly how much money is siphoned from people who are probably too gullible to be put in front of their own email (some would say that if you are stupid enough to believe David Miliband is going to invest £40 million in you, then you don't deserve to have money in the first place), but the figure for the UK, according to Chatham House, is around £150 million per year – or about £31,000 per dupe, they say.

The desire to get rich without working for it tempts all of us. But the people who are making the big money are usually the tempters, not the tempted.

Treat emails from strangers offering you lottery prizes in the same way as you would someone who walked up to you in the street with the same proposition. Walk on by.

3 BE A CONTRARIAN

Extraordinary Popular Delusions **may well have remained a quirky-yet-obscure Victorian compendium of trivia if it were not for the involvement of an American financier called Bernard Baruch, who understood the madness of crowds perfectly.**

Having been introduced to the book by a journalist in middle age, Baruch kept his well-thumbed copy at home, and credited it with having a huge influence on his professional behaviour.

DEFINING IDEA...

When good news about the market hits the front page of the New York Times, *sell.*
– BERNARD BARUCH

So, by means of repaying the debt, Baruch wrote the foreword to the 1932 edition of the book. In it he credited *Extraordinary Popular Delusions* as being the inspiration behind his decision to sell all his stock just before the financial crash of 1929. Why? Because everyone he consulted during 1929 about the markets said that nothing could possibly go wrong.

Baruch is also the reason that the first three chapters of the book, just a small fraction of the words contained in the whole, are the ones that are most often read and admired. They deal with 'bubbles' – the financial panics when everyone wants to get into something good, and people usually pay so much that they end up broke as a result when it goes sour.

He is, however, only the most famous of a sub-group of market traders that Mackay would very much have admired: the contrarians. Their philosophy is to look for value by betting against the market, rather than following it. They buy in unfashionable markets, they invest in companies that are at rock bottom and they sell when it's all going too well to fail.

One of the greatest contrarians of the modern age is Anthony Bolton, who built Fidelity's Special Situations Fund into a £3 billion juggernaut while it was under his stewardship. However, he's not a superstar 'Gordon Gekko' trader. His cautious and sustained growth strategy led to a 14,700% rise in value over thirty years for the fund he administered. 'I get it right about three times out of five,' he says. 'I'm a contrarian: when everyone loves something, I shy away from it. When everyone hates something, I want to look at it.'

He adds the advice that even if you follow the crowd into the stock market, you don't have to follow them out of it if – or when – a bear market comes along. That would often be compounding the error. When everyone runs for the hills, if the fundamentals of your investment are sound, the stocks will recover – and you don't want someone else to pick up that profit. 'A lot of investors get sucked into markets when they're good and shaken out when they are bad,' he says, adding 'My advice is to hold on.'

HERE'S AN IDEA FOR YOU...

If you want a cheap demonstration of how being a contrarian can make you cash, try sports betting on an exchange (like a mini stock market) such as Betfair. A team loses twice, and thousands of people bet on it for relegation. Then it wins, and everyone bets on the other teams instead. Simply by betting against the crowd, you can profit.

4 20/20 HINDSIGHT

We look back on the past as some kind of inevitable chain of cause and effect that could only lead to where we are now.

We are, by nature, deterministic. We reinterpret the past in the context of what we know now – so even when we try, we can't escape from our personal delusions.

DEFINING IDEA...

Fortune brings in some boats that are not steered.

~ WILLIAM SHAKESPEARE

Chapter 1 of Mackay's book involves one of the oddest mass delusions of recent history, the Mississippi Scheme, which not only ruined many people but also brought an entire country to its knees. Yet right at the beginning, Mackay takes care to point out that the man who set the Scheme in motion – a Scot named John Law – was not a 'knave or a madman', and was 'more sinned against than sinning'. He understood that when we point the finger, we usually wait until after the event.

There's a lot to explain about the Mississippi Scheme, but in outline it's enough to know that Law had the idea that the French government should sell stock in the Mississippi Company, a French creation which had the trading rights in that part of the world. Thanks to a combination of circumstances, the public were so keen on the paper which was issued that during 1719 and 1720 the clamour to buy sent the price rocketing upwards – and then just as swiftly shooting downwards again. At that point, the government was unable to pay everyone who wanted to sell.

Lives were ruined. People were crushed in the panic and murdered for money. Law, not surprisingly, was public enemy number one. He, however, wasn't some international con artist. He didn't set out to create a panic. He had bright ideas and principles, which were twisted by those in the French government who wished to increase their profits from the scheme.

Similarly, today we do the same for failures in business – and we attribute the opposite characteristics to successful leaders. Those who fail, we assume, had deep flaws. On the other hand those who succeeded must have been smarter and stronger. An example: Microsoft wasn't IBM's first choice to create its computer operating system; at this time, Bill Gates got lucky. He might have proved to be very smart and a great CEO, but had IBM's decision been different would he still have been a billionaire? Probably not.

When we get too hung up on outcomes, we reinterpret what led to them as if there was an inevitability in the chain of cause and effect, and as if there was always a person to blame or credit.

People are usually neither as clever or as dumb as we assume, based on what they achieved. The idea that every occurrence, good or bad, can be attributed to a hero or villain is the biggest delusion of all.

HERE'S AN IDEA FOR YOU...

Sometimes bad things happen to good people. When you review projects that went wrong, make it a search for the truth – not a search for someone to blame.

5 FUNDAMENTALLY WRONG

In his chronicle of the Mississippi Scheme, Mackay reminds us of something that we often forget: a valuation placed on future potential is only supportable as long as people believe that potential.

DEFINING IDEA...

The strongest arguments prove nothing so long as the conclusions are not verified by experience.
~ ROGER BACON

When Law set up the Mississippi Company, he saw to it that it was granted exclusive rights to levy taxes and issue money. The area it covered was rumoured to 'abound in the precious metals', and the regent of France also conferred on the company the sole right to sell tobacco and refine gold and silver.

Initially, Law was cautious in his valuation of the company. He issued shares in it to a value of sixty million livres – quite enough to make it a spectacular money generator for the French state, but sadly not enough to satisfy all the investors. So the regent, who had incorporated the company into the Royal Bank of France, issued notes to a value of one billion livres. Yearly dividends were promised at a rate of 120%.

What no one quite thought through in the frenzy to invest was that there was, in the year following the establishment of the company, no trade – just the right to trade. There were no profits, just promises. There was no gold and silver and tobacco, yet, to generate the cash from which profits could be paid.

We could kid ourselves that such a thing could never happen now, but in the last 300 years such speculation has been as widespread as ever. Those who lived through the investment madness of the dot-com boom might recall it well, and might also recall that some of the people who believed the hype weren't peasants or financial novices.

One of my friends at the time ran an agency that handled the publicity for the stars of the dot-com boom, the young paper gazillionaires who ten years ago didn't just fill the business pages, but the news and style pages too. Her company – which was turning away business – grew rapidly until it occupied two floors of a huge office building. Then, abruptly, the agency collapsed.

Instead of fees, she had taken payment from her clients by taking a stake in their young and exciting companies. As long as investor confidence in them held up, so did the business which was built on taking a slice of the value that confidence had created.

When the confidence disappeared, my friend found that she had massive overheads and many slices of next to nothing. The confidence disappeared almost overnight when the big investors realised that while these businesses might have been good ideas, few were making – or ever would make – enough money to repay the investment.

Now we can see that the investment was made on the basis of little more than optimistic speculation. When all that optimism collapses, so does everything else.

HERE'S AN IDEA FOR YOU...

You can't tell if something is working unless you measure it. Set a return on investment for your projects to make a contribution, with a deadline. Monitor the progress towards that at monthly intervals.

6 INVESTMENTS CAN GO DOWN

A good idea is often only good in the time and the place for which it was created. The idea that speculation is a one-way bet is a delusion, and often a costly one.

Law was simply creating a structure that we're all familiar with today (and as shareholders, we're all part of). Law declared that 'a banker deserved death if he made issues without having sufficient security to answer all demands'. If that were true today, bank offices would be death row.

DEFINING IDEA...

Another great evil arising from this desire ...not to be thought poor, is the destructive thing which has been honoured by the name of 'speculation'; but which ought to be called Gambling.

~ WILLIAM COBBETT

The problem for the Mississippi Scheme wasn't failure, but spectacular success. Thousands flocked to subscribe and prices for the notes shot through the roof, then speculators who bought and sold got rich very quickly. The government profited too, and that lay behind the decision of the Duke of Orleans to extend the Scheme (he was running the country as regent, because the King was seven years old and so not up with the latest financial instruments).

He should have known that simply doubling the number of notes might double profits in the short term, but in the long term would lead to disaster – as it did, when confidence in the Mississippi Company collapsed and the notes plunged in value as everyone tried to turn their paper back into coin.

And so it is today. If you haven't been living under a rock for the last couple of years, you might have heard that property values have been falling. At the heart of this is the British obsession that you can't lose by investing in property – so more people want to invest.

In a limited way, this is healthy. A strong housing market, more home ownership, solid long-term investment…

But banks forgot their discipline. In the past, they lent money reluctantly, when they were sure there was little risk; homeowners got a small but regular return. By 2005 house prices were rocketing, so they sometimes lent more than the value of the house that secured the loan, and could lend to high-risk customers because the value of the house would far exceed the value of the loan secured on it. It seems a virtuous circle – until the banks realised that they couldn't carry all the risky loans they had been writing. They stopped lending money.

So fewer people could get a mortgage. When there are few buyers and many sellers, prices fall. When prices fall, fewer people can sell their houses to buy another one, because they can't pay back the money they borrowed. The market collapses, because it has been underpinned not by tangible assets but by the greed of speculators. It's a miniature Mississippi Scheme, 300 years later, and in our own back yards.

HERE'S AN IDEA FOR YOU...

Insurance reduces your profit in any transaction, but it eliminates the chance of disaster. In good times, we omit to insure ourselves, our houses, our families, our business deals. Now's the time to cut down on the speculation. You can't make a profit if you're out of business.

7 SELL TOO SOON

Bubbles are times when there's a lot of cash to be had – for a short time.

Financial bubbles like the Mississippi Scheme release large amounts of what, in the jargon, we ought to call liquidity: spending money. People take their money from the bank to invest; money passes between buyers and sellers; the people who get wealthy start to throw their money around; the people who think they are about to get wealthy do the same, even if they don't quite have the money yet, because others are willing to give them credit based on their new-found wealth.

It's a fun time for all. Apart from the basic excitement of making a fast buck, a society or culture that had got a bit samey suddenly bursts into life. 'It was remarked at this time,' Mackay says, 'that Paris had never before been so full of objects of elegance and luxury. Statues, pictures and tapestries were imported in great quantities from foreign countries, and found a ready market.' The elite in France used their gains to rebuild houses, buy horses and generally patch up their finances.

It's one thing to be rich. It's quite another to live the life, and large portions of the country whose life had (until now) been devoid of tapestries and statues, were indeed living it: 'All those pretty trifles in the way of furniture and ornament which the French excel in manufacturing were no longer the exclusive playthings of the aristocracy, but were to be found in the houses of traders and the middle classes in general.'

When there was cash to be made, everybody who made cash shared in the pot. An old man's servant was sent to sell stock at 8000 livres, but by the time he got to the Jardin de Soissons where the sales took place, the price was 10,000. He pocketed the difference and left the country. Law's own coachman quickly made enough to retire, and did.

Some of the smarter people in the market, like the old man's servant, decided that they should take their profits in the lowest risk form available. That meant getting it far away from any economic threat that could destroy it. Mackay tells of one stock-jobber who gradually converted all his gain to cash, and sent it out of the country in a farm cart. Others bought precious metals and fine art, which again they shipped away.

From the moment someone takes his or her profit out of the system that created it, liquidity begins to dry up. When that happens, there are sellers of a commodity but not buyers – and when that happens, prices plunge. You need to be in the first tranche of profit-takers. As Bernard Baruch, the financier who popularised *Extraordinary Popular Delusions* in the twentieth century said: 'I made my money by selling too soon.'

HERE'S AN IDEA FOR YOU...

When you're winning, move some of your profits into something with little risk – like cash. Gamble with money you've won, not with money you need. The same applies in investment or roulette.

8 THE KING IS IN THE ALTOGETHER

When your point of view goes against the grain, people don't tend to disagree with your point of view. They attack you personally. It's safer, though usually wrong, to go with the flow.

DEFINING IDEA...

If you never change your mind, why have one?

~ EDWARD DE BONO

One of the few notable French citizens to publicly proclaim that the Mississippi Scheme was barmy was the old soldier Marshal Villars. In the normal run of things he would have been respected or admired by the crowd, but one day, Mackay tells us, he decided to stop his carriage in the Place Vendome, where the crowds gathered to buy and sell (mostly to try to buy) stock in the Mississippi Company. 'Putting his head out of the carriage window, he harangued them for full half an hour on their "disgusting avarice",' he tells us.

The crowd, as you can guess, were not best pleased, and hissed and mocked the old Marshal. When they started to attack the carriage he drove on and never went back.

Mackay also tells of two intellectuals who used to meet regularly and congratulate each other on having nothing to do with the Scheme – until one day they bumped into each other at the entrance to the Hotel de Soissons, where one was going in to buy shares, and the other was coming out having already bought them.

It's never a comfortable feeling to be the one person in the room who disagrees with the mob. We all know the story of the Emperor's new clothes, and we quote it approvingly to each other – but usually after the fact. We're all brave with hindsight, when we can say, 'I knew there was a problem there' or 'I could tell there was nothing in it'.

When was the sub-prime lending problem spotted? In the three years from the middle of 2005 to the middle of 2008 there were around 40,000 newspaper articles published with the phrase 'sub-prime [or subprime] crisis'. Before the middle of 2005, there were barely half a dozen. Does this mean that no one had spotted the problem? We assume not, as those half a dozen tended to be more serious, weighty pieces in which the modern-day Marshal Villarses warned of the danger to the global financial system, and to the lending banks. They were too obscure for the popular newspapers, and you can imagine how those who were pulling down seven-figure bonuses at that time must have scoffed at the idea that they were involved in an enterprise that might plunge much of the developed world into recession.

Still, they're hopefully out of a job now, so maybe next time they will listen.

But will they? The point of the Emperor's new clothes is that we like to appear clever when really we're just following the crowd. When that crowd has more money than us (the modern way of measuring success), we're even more tempted. Probably it's better to accept that few of us have the independence of mind and bravery to be Marshal Villars.

HERE'S AN IDEA FOR YOU...

Don't just ask 'why?' when things are going wrong, but question success as well. Asking hard questions isn't negative; if there's money involved, it's compulsory.

9 BLAME SOMEONE

John Law took the blame for almost ruining France with the Mississippi Scheme. When we blame someone else, it often means we don't have to accept responsibility for our own stupidity.

When there's a crisis, we look for a scapegoat. It's natural. Someone has to be responsible. And it's easier to blame someone else than it is to blame ourselves.

DEFINING IDEA...
You can't cheat an honest man.
~ W. C. FIELDS

'When Law, by the utter failure of his best laid plans, rendered himself obnoxious, satire of course seized upon him... many of these songs were far from decent; and one of them in particular counselled the application of all his notes to the most ignoble use to which paper can be applied,' says Mackay. But Law had worse problems than a people singing a few bawdy songs. When he travelled anywhere he had to go in disguise or under the King's protection. Eventually he fled the country, to the huge displeasure of all the people who wanted to see him hang.

While we don't fully understand what keeps causing economic bubbles, we can be pretty sure that they can't be pinned on the actions of any one person. In experiments even well-regulated markets, ones which haven't been distorted by any person or act, and in which otherwise well-educated and sensible people are trading, experience bubbles. Whatever the madness is, it's a madness inherent in all of us.

One of the purest speculative bubbles of the twentieth century also shows our general tendency to blame someone for the consequences. When Charles Ponzi emigrated from Italy to Boston, Massachusetts in 1903, he was a bad gambler and a chancer. By 1920 he had created the greatest mass speculation of his era, and bankrupted six banks.

The Ponzi Scheme was simple. Ponzi noted that international postal reply coupons could be redeemed in the US for more than they cost in Europe. He set up a company promising to exploit this discrepancy, and sold stock in it for $10, promising investors 50% interest in only ninety days. People were soon queuing up to buy massive amounts of the stock.

Ponzi was paying interest to his early investors from the sums deposited by the later investors. In a few months the whole thing came crashing down, but not before many of Boston's richest, most important or cleverest citizens had queued up to invest in it. Today, any business that pays benefits to subscribers from the deposits of later subscribers is known by Ponzi's name. Well, not quite any: that's what the state pension does.

Blaming one person might make us feel better, but looking more closely at our own motivations might be a better route to take if we want to avoid being fooled again.

HERE'S AN IDEA FOR YOU...

When you're investing, by all means look at the daily price shifts for entertainment and mild speculation, but make sure the majority of your portfolio is geared to offering long-term returns. Over ten or twenty years a conservative investment is far more attractive than a meteoric stock.

10 A VERY BRITISH BUBBLE

If you think that financial manias are a foreign affliction, the South Sea Bubble shows that Brits can go just as crazy as any French person when there's a profit to be had.

DEFINING IDEA...

He could not calculate the madness of people.

~ JOSEPH SPENCE, ANECDOTES ~ SIR ISAAC NEWTON'S RESPONSE TO THE QUESTION OF HOW HIGH SOUTH SEA STOCK WOULD RISE (HIS NIECE LATER SAID THAT HE LOST £20,000).

The story of the South Sea Company shows how a sensible notion (rather like Law's idea) can career off the rails. The South Sea Company was set up in 1711 as a way to pay off the public debt through trade. It was granted a monopoly of trade to the South Seas (nowadays South America), which seemed a very fine idea all round. The world was being discovered, trade was mushrooming, so adventurous men could make a profit.

Our reticent national character is perhaps at its worst when we're over-excited. Gold and silver mines were spoken of in South America. And '… everyone believed them to be inexhaustible, and that it was only necessary to send the manufactures of England to the coast to be repaid a hundredfold in gold and silver ingots by the natives,' as Mackay says.

The trade with South America never came to very much (disagreements with Spain saw to that), but in 1720, at about the time the French were going Mississippi mad, the British went South Sea stupid. The South Sea Company was surviving as a sort of de facto investment bank, and was at the time in competition with the Bank of England. When the South Sea Company offered to pay off a large chunk of the national debt at extravagant terms, and the Chancellor of the Exchequer supported the idea, a frenzy of investment in the company began. The public swapped government debt for shares in the company, which were promised to yield fantastic returns – just as soon as all that gold and silver came in.

By August 1720 the frenzy of speculation in the South Sea Company had driven the stock price from £130 to £1000, from which it swiftly (and inevitably) collapsed, just as all the bubbles did.

What was specifically British about the rise and fall of the South Sea Company?

Perhaps it was the way in which the Establishment at once lined their pockets, promoted the scheme and looked after each other. Politicians could buy shares in the scheme, but they didn't have to shell out hard cash. They simply took the shares that were offered and sold them when the price went up. The company then sent them their profit. Not surprisingly, the scheme had many supporters in parliament, and the idea that so many eminent investors were convinced of its worth increased the frenzy of the common people to get some shares for themselves.

When the share price collapsed, ruining many families, destroying businesses and almost bankrupting the country, one of the politicians who had been making money from the company in this way was discovered to be Mr Aislabie, the Chancellor.

HERE'S AN IDEA FOR YOU...

Have a code of conduct in your business that makes sure personal relationships aren't abused. Every substantial deal should be checked by a third party if you want to make sure that personal relationships are a positive influence on your sales performance.

11 DON'T BELIEVE THE HYPE

As Mackay points out, one of the reasons the South Sea Bubble inflated so dramatically and quickly was the power of rumour.

DEFINING IDEA...

If I'd gone around saying 'We'll probably get through this,' no one would have printed anything.

– ROBIN GUENIER
HEAD OF TASKFORCE 2000

As the Bill to create the South Sea Company made its two-month progress through the House of Commons, the cautious speeches of the politicians who disapproved of the speculation were drowned out in the public ear by fantastic rumours of a treaty between Spain and England, '...and the rich produce of the mines of Potosi-le-Paz was to be brought to England until silver should become almost as plentiful as iron'. In the House of Lords 'several peers spoke warmly against the scheme; but their warnings fell on dull, cold ears... the whole nation had turned stock-jobbers'.

The people who invested in the scheme were not stupid; they were not all naive in business. But one attribute that they almost all shared was that they heard their information second-hand from a group of people who had a direct interest that they should be believed. Nor were all of the people who originated the story cynical. They might have believed in the fabulous potential of the mines of Mexico. The Spanish mined about 5000 tonnes of silver from Potosi (it's in Bolivia. And very poor, because the silver was shipped out – to Spain).

It's a lesson that rumour tends to exaggerate a story. It's exactly the same today. The best example in recent years was the Millennium Bug, the supposed failure of computer systems as the date changed from 1999 to 2000. When the early prophets of potential doom were ignored, they – fearing widespread catastrophe – stoked up the message. This was carried by a group of people who stood to benefit greatly from consultancy work, and an unquestioning media who repeated possibilities of global financial collapse, hospital heart monitors failing and 'riots, terrorism and a health crisis' (*Sunday Mirror*) as simple fact. The best retelling of the Y2K non-disaster, and a savage indictment of the way that newspapers sometimes turn rumour into fact, is found in *Flat Earth News*, by Nick Davies.

Eventually, as we know, the 'Y2K meltdown' never occurred. I have to admit an interest. As a journalist who had written many Y2K stories, I was contracted in 1999 to help research a TV documentary on the subject. My job: to chase down the stories of potential disaster and establish the facts. When I attempted to do that, most of the stories were little more than urban myths. The weight of the evidence existed mostly in the fact that everyone believed the exaggerated version retold by non-experts.

The problem is that there's more rumour dressed up as fact than ever these days. Sometimes we call it inside information. Sometimes we call it 24-hour news. Often we mistakenly call it 'evidence'. But, as everyone who lost out in the South Sea Bubble would have told you, be careful who you believe. When you're told something by someone who heard that it was true, examine the motives of the rumour-mongers before you believe them.

HERE'S AN IDEA FOR YOU...

Rumour is corrosive in a business. A weekly clear-the-air meeting – where anyone can anonymously submit a question – can stop people acting on unreliable information.

12 PAST PERFORMANCE

First the bad news: it looks as if we are genetically programmed to over-react.

I can't think of any good news that's directly relevant to this, except the good news that now we're all aware of it, we can try to put some kind of mechanism in place to mitigate the effects.

DEFINING IDEA...

If you can react the same way to winning and losing, that's a big accomplishment.

~ CHRIS EVERT

Without the tendency to over-react, stock market bubbles wouldn't be much of a problem. In the midst of the South Sea Bubble, there appeared in Exchange Alley 'Globe Permits'. These permits were square pieces of card, on which there was the seal of the Globe Tavern. 'The possessors enjoyed no other advantage from them than permission to subscribe at some future time to a new sail-cloth manufactury... these permits sold for as much as sixty guineas,' Mackay relates.

Let's back up a bit here: a piece of cardboard, promising its bearer a stake in a company that didn't exist, sold for a sum equivalent to thousands of pounds today, simply because the originator was identified with the South Sea Company. It's mind-boggling, but an example of how our minds can be boggled.

Whatever the evolutionary reason for this (and you can imagine how over-reaction to danger might be a good idea), the principle of reacting based on recent stimuli is a key component of bad decision-making. It's one that economists are just beginning to break open. An example is the recent work that has been done by the economists Thierry Post, Martijn Van Den Assem, Guido Baltussen and Richard Thaler – who is one of the leading thinkers in what is being called 'behavioural economics' – on the decisions made by contestants in a TV quiz show.

Those of you who have watched *Deal or No Deal*, probably when you're pretending to work from home, will know that there's no real skill attached to the show. Contestants simply decide which boxes to eliminate. Some have high-value cash prizes, some have low-value prizes. They either finish with a single box (their prize) or accept an offer from the quizmaster based on the value of the remaining boxes.

You would think that contestants would add up the value of the prizes on offer and use that to weight their decisions. Not so.

'Contrary to the traditional view of expected utility theory, the choices can be explained in large part by previous outcomes experienced during the game,' the researchers have found. Put simply, we're driving by looking in the rear view mirror. Contestants that get lucky early take risky choices later.

The idea that we take risks based on previous outcomes rather than doing the most basic analysis to discover whether history is actually any guide to the future is a flaw in our programming – and, as stock market bubbles show, it's a dangerous flaw.

HERE'S AN IDEA FOR YOU...

How many of your decisions are based on 'It worked last time'? Take another look, and you might see that some of those successful outcomes are random, or – even worse – lucky.

13 ALL-IN ECONOMICS

If you want to know how not to speculate, learn it from a bad poker player.

There's a big danger in comparing playing a game with rules and well-understood chances to a poorly understood phenomenon like an economic bubble, but I will anyway, because there are some useful parallels to be drawn.

DEFINING IDEA...

Poker exemplifies the worst aspects of capitalism that have made our country so great.

~ WALTER MATTHAU

At the height of the South Sea Bubble Mackay points out that 'Persons of distinction, of both sexes, were deeply engaged in all these bubbles; those of the male sex going to taverns and coffee houses to meet their brokers, and the ladies resorting for the same purpose to the shops of milliners and haberdashers. But it did not follow that all these people believed in the feasibility of the schemes to which they subscribed; it was enough for their purposes that their shares would, by stock-jobbing arts, be soon raised to a premium.'

This seems an entirely reasonable thing to do when shares could be bought at one end of Exchange Alley and sold for 10% more at the other end. But for anyone who plays poker today, the flaw in this idea is immediately apparent.

The problem is that by mindlessly betting on a winning streak, you'll win repeatedly – until you lose. And while you win small amounts, you lose big.

In poker tournaments there's a naive strategy that you don't need to know the rules of poker to understand. You can, in no-limit poker, bet all your chips at once; it's called going 'all in'. It usually signifies to others that you have an almost unbeatable hand – a sure thing – and most of the time the other players, who have made small bets, will give up their bets so that they don't have to go all in and compete with you, because if they lose, they're out of the game. So you usually win a few small bets from them, even when you secretly know that your cards weren't very good.

Some players get the idea that this is infallible. They keep pushing all their chips in, whatever their cards, and after twenty minutes they are well ahead because no one takes them on. Eventually, though, our reckless gambler is pretty much guaranteed to come up against someone who is sure that he or she has better cards, who will match the bet, and take all our gambler's chips. And she or he's lost everything.

When we use the past record of winning investments as our only guide to profit through speculation (rather than the quality of the investment), we're taking the same risk. You copy the winners, you win. You have even more confidence to repeat what you did, you win, and so do your friends who copy you. You have more confidence, you commit even more – and you all lose.

HERE'S AN IDEA FOR YOU...

A good poker player plays every hand on its merits, and evaluates all the variables in every situation. So does a good trader. Bad traders copy the good ones, but they don't know why. Really bad traders copy the bad ones. Don't copy anyone.

14 BEWARE OF IMITATION

The South Sea Company had many imitators, all with about as much chance of success for investors as the original.

DEFINING IDEA...

We are all easily taught to imitate what is base and depraved.

– JUVENAL

As the South Sea Company's fortunes soared, it's hardly surprising that other people should have thought that the idea of launching a joint stock company similar in construction – but with some other exciting way to earn money – would be a great idea. And so it happened. 'Some of them lasted for a week, or a fortnight, and were no more heard of,' says Mackay, stating 'there were nearly a hundred different projects, each more extravagant and deceptive than the other.'

Some of these projects were neatly targeted. A company for 'encouraging the breed of horses in England, and of improving of glebe and church lands, and repairing and rebuilding parsonage and vicarage houses' was aimed at wealthy fox-hunting parsons, Mackay points out. It was well subscribed, so many of those parsons were a little less wealthy when the bubble burst.

Among the other South Sea imitators were companies for 'improving of gardens', for 'drying malt by hot air', for 'extracting silver from lead' and for 'the art of making soap'. One printmaker created a pack of cards with each card dedicated to making fun of another bubble company that had sought (and sometimes found) investors.

The best example of bubble craziness was the unknown man who created 'A company for carrying on the undertaking of great advantage, but nobody knows what it is'. Nobody does to this day, but the prospectus stated that he required £500,000, and was selling 5000 shares at £100 each. To get the shares, you needed to pay a £2 deposit, and would get £100 a year per share. When this man opened his office 'crowds of people beset his doors, and when he shut up at three o'clock, he found that no less than one thousand shares had been subscribed for'.

He had made £2000 – a small fortune in those days – and bunked off to the continent the same evening, '…and was never heard from again'.

When the investment bug bites, people don't just make terrible investments, they rush to copy each other's terrible ideas. And, for a short time, investors also rush to throw money at them. Here's a more modern example. In the dot-com boom, a company called Flooz.com raised $35 million in investment. The idea was that you use your credit card to buy 'Flooz', which you then use to pay for things. So it's like a credit card, only it takes longer, and you need to pay for your Flooz on a credit card anyway. And here's the kicker: even Flooz had imitators that got funded.

HERE'S AN IDEA FOR YOU…

If you're not the lowest-price producer in your market, you need to be different, and that differentiation by definition needs to be uncopiable. So now is the time to take a fresh look at what you do that's impossible for your competitors to copy, and develop the value of it.

15 FLOWER POWER

The third of the three economic bubbles Mackay writes about is the strangest of the lot. What makes people pay a fortune for a tulip?

DEFINING IDEA...

Showing off is the fool's idea of glory.

– BRUCE LEE

The French and British might have gone bananas over the potential of speculative companies, but at least some of the investors thought there might have been something to trade that had value beyond the price of the stock. A century earlier the Dutch had created their own economic bubble that made the South Sea Bubble seem almost sensible. They went mad for tulips.

Mackay's account of the Tulipomania is entertaining, but it has to be taken with a pinch of salt. He did his research second-hand, based on the writings of people who were firmly against speculation. We'll get to that later. He alleges that the bubble caused the ruin of many people, and there's not much evidence to show that, either. But we do know this: in the 1630s the price of tulips shot up and then crashed, and some of the investors lost a lot of money.

Why tulips? It's a good example of one of the foundations of economics: scarcity. The drivers for demand for whatever is scarce might be basic need (for example, water scarcity), but are also peer pressure and the desire for approval (fashion or the need to look clever and well connected).

'The rage for possessing them [tulips] soon caught the middle classes of society, and merchants and shopkeepers, even of moderate means, began to vie with each other in the rarity of these flowers,' Mackay says. In his account, one of the two bulbs of Semper Augustus was sold in 1636 for twelve acres of building ground; the other for 4600 florins, a carriage, two grey horses and a complete suit of harness. A florin at that time is equivalent to about £7 today. Some of this was undoubtedly so the buyers could show off to their colleagues their success in commerce – rather like the posh neighbour who insists on taking you for a drive in his expensive new car.

Sometimes prudent people are fooled if they are in too much of a hurry to get some of the action. The *Wall Street Journal* published a famous list in 1973 of the investors in the Home-Stake Production Company, a simple fraud that promised subscribers that it was drilling for oil (it wasn't), and promised a 400% return plus tax deductions on their investment if they got in early. It was a basic Ponzi Scheme; they were paying early subscribers from the subscriptions they got later.

Almost 3000 of the wealthiest people in the US were fooled. David Cassidy, Mia Farrow, several senators, the president of Columbia University, Walter Matthau and a former Secretary of Defense were all in the very long list. They didn't need the money. They also had plenty of opportunities to check up on the company. They were too busy getting in on the action to bother.

HERE'S AN IDEA FOR YOU...

Think: it makes you feel good to be in on the action, to be part of a chosen few who can speculate and to play the part, but would you invest in this opportunity if no one knew you were investing? It's an expensive way to show off.

16 ESCAPE THE CROWD

Tulipomania was a local fashion, as later were speculations on the South Seas and the Mississippi. What can cause a mass panic in one country causes hardly a raised eyebrow in another.

DEFINING IDEA...

The intelligence of the creature known as a crowd is the square root of the number of people in it.

– TERRY PRATCHETT

The chicness of tulips in seventeenth-century Haarlem and Amsterdam isn't in doubt. 'It was deemed a proof of bad taste in any man of fortune to be without a collection of them,' says Mackay, as he struggles to explain exactly why it was the tulip, which at that time suffered from disease and was difficult to transplant and cultivate, that so captivated the Dutch. Eventually he decided it was because the flower was such a weakling: 'Many persons grow insensibly attached to that which gives them a great deal of trouble, as a mother often loves her sick and ever ailing child better than her more healthy offspring.'

But this goes to show how localised the fashion was. In France, people liked tulips well enough, and they had some fashion value, but the rise in their price was short-lived. So too for London, where by the time Mackay was writing a gardener on King's Road in Chelsea had a tulip offered at 200 guineas, but 'the jobbers exerted themselves to the utmost to raise them to the fictitious value they had acquired in Amsterdam,' and notably failed.

When we look at the history of bubbles and other crowd madnesses, they rarely travel. Stock market gains are sometimes an exception – but only because in Western Europe we share the same institutions, financial instruments and news with the US. Even so, while stock markets may follow each other, as sentiment is globalised, it's not always the case.

Outside of finance, it's remarkable just how often mass panics, speculations and delusions are strictly bounded. It may be that they match something in the national character, or it may just be that we transmit our mass hysteria best through personal contact. Whatever the reason, crowd behaviour is usually local.

An example comes from Ben Goldacre's excellent 'Bad Science' column in the *Guardian*, which regularly skewers the worst examples of shoddy science and mass panics. It's required reading if you don't want to become unwittingly caught in crowd madness.

Goldacre has long been the most vocal and considered critic of the mass panic around the MMR vaccine. As he points out in his book (also called *Bad Science*), 'The MMR and autism scare… is practically non-existent outside Britain.' He has been one of the few voices in the UK press to consistently point out that there is no basis in science to connect the MMR vaccine to autism.

Instead, other countries have their own obsessions. In the 1990s, large numbers of French people were convinced that the Hepatitis B vaccine caused multiple sclerosis. In the US, a preservative called thiomersalin used in vaccines is under mass suspicion, even though few people outside the country have even heard of it.

HERE'S AN IDEA FOR YOU...

Don't rely exclusively on local sources for commentary on business. Add international news and information sources to your browser. If you're inside a bubble, they might offer you the view from outside it.

17 GOING TO ABILENE

Bubbles often depend on groupthink: the ability of a crowd to make a decision, collectively, that no single member of the group would have reached on their own.

Mackay's version of tulipomania, whether it's an accurate history or a caricature created from unreliable testimony, still serves as an example of 'groupthink' – where a group reaches a consensus that is potentially damaging (as this one certainly was) because no one challenges the dynamics of the group at the time.

Tulipomania is not a pure example of groupthink, as it involves (as we have seen) basic economic forces, as well as the potential for profit. But unlike the Mississippi Scheme and the South Sea Bubble, there is little evidence of widespread speculation. Instead, a group of buyers became convinced of the extraordinary value of a flower.

DEFINING IDEA...

Brian: You're all individuals!
Crowd (as one): Yes, we're all
individuals!
Brian: You're all different!
Crowd (as one): Yes, we are
all different!
Man: I'm not.
~ 'MONTY PYTHON'S LIFE OF BRIAN'

If you had consulted any single member of the group of purchasers of tulip bulbs before the mania began and asked them whether twenty acres of land was a suitable price for any single tulip bulb, they'd have said no. But as the group consensus changed, they went along. We don't know much about the aftermath – despite Mackay's assertion that 'the cry of distress resounded everywhere', there's little hard evidence that many merchants were ruined – but once the groupthink consensus was broken, it's reasonable to assume that many Dutch taverns were inhabited by merchants scratching their heads and wondering what they had been thinking, at least.

Groupthink is a surprisingly common and powerful force in decision making. For example, take the Abilene Paradox. This is a term coined by management expert Jerry B. Harvey in 1974. Harvey's example is this: a family is holidaying in Texas. One afternoon the father-in-law suggests visiting the town of Abilene, fifty-three miles away, for dinner. The wife says it sounds like a great idea, her husband agrees (despite having reservations, he doesn't want to rock the boat), and his mother also agrees. They drive to Abilene, have a terrible dinner, and drive back. All four reveal that they didn't really want to go, but they all agreed because they thought the others wanted to make the trip.

The paradox is that when a group reaches a decision, it can sometimes be an outcome that no single member of the group would support. Whether it's your niece going crazy for a TV show that she admits she never liked six months later, your co-workers all deciding that they ought to have a Christmas party that no one really wants, or the board deciding to hire an idiot that it turns out no one wants either, groupthink has been influencing crowds as long as two or three people have gathered together – long before meetings, tulips or Abilene existed.

HERE'S AN IDEA FOR YOU...

If you want to avoid groupthink, there are plenty of ways to do it. Invite outsiders who know about a project to share their opinions and be questioned, but don't invite yes men, and keep an open mind. The more your critics irritate you with their objections, the better.

18 PUMP AND DUMP

South Sea Company stock had a little help in maintaining its price – the directors engaged in every type of scheme to keep prices rising.

DEFINING IDEA...

It is a far, far better thing to have a firm anchor in nonsense than to put out on the troubled seas of thought.

~ JOHN KENNETH GALBRAITH

Throughout 1720, the South Sea Company had done everything possible to prop up the stock price, knowing that once it started to fall, the game was up (without trade revenues, there really wasn't much else to the South Sea Company except its stock price). This included the excellent ruse of lending money to people so that they could buy stock in the company, of holding a public meeting when the stock fell at which the eminent (and stock-holding) men of the day would speak in favour of the South Sea Company, and all manner of rumours and insinuations.

Dishonest (or at best amoral) people can get away with this sort of behaviour when we're all so obsessed by the prospect of a quick profit that we are prepared to believe anything, and to look the other way when we suspect something is not quite right. 'The public mind was in a state of unwholesome fermentation,' writes Mackay. 'Men were no longer satisfied with the slow but sure profits of cautious industry.'

The dishonourable tactics used by the desperate directors of the South Sea Company, and others, are still commonplace. One of the growth sectors in the organised crime business, for example, is 'pump and dump'.

It works like this: fraudsters circulate emails and post messages on bulletin boards to say that a microcap stock (one where even a small number of buyers will make the share price rise, and about which there's little independent information) is on the rise and you need to buy quickly to ensure your profit. You check the price, and it's rising – but only because of the actions of fellow punters like you. Naive punters often put their entire life savings into something like this, because the pump puts their mind into a state of unwholesome fermentation.

After pumping the stock, the fraudsters – who bought it at the bottom – make huge profits by selling their cheap stock to you and me.

How easy is it to pump and dump today? Very. One of the most celebrated schemes was run by Jonathan Lebed, who bought stocks, talked them up and then sold them at a profit between September 1999 and February 2000. He signed on to bulletin boards under false names and talked up the stock, and then cashed in. His lowest daily return was $12,000. Eventually he settled with the Securities and Exchange Commission and repaid $285,000 – which left him with at least $500,000 of profit for about six months work.

Lebed, at the time, was fifteen years old.

HERE'S AN IDEA FOR YOU...

It's a good policy to have two independent sources of information for any investment decision. Make it a rule in your business.

19 SURVIVOR BIAS

When investment bubbles occur everyone seems to be doing well, and they're desperate to tell you about it in the pub, at work and in the newspapers. But it's another demonstration that history is written by the winners.

DEFINING IDEA...

There are no winners, only survivors.

~ FRANK GIFFORD, AMERICAN FOOTBALL PLAYER

In his excellent book *Fooled by Randomness*, which is about as effective a counterpoint to the temptation to invest in short-term bubbles as it's possible to read, trader Nassim Nicholas Taleb points out that the 'star' traders in any market are the ones suited to the prevailing conditions. Mackay raises a similar point when he points out that the English had a model for how not to create a joint-stock company directly across the English Channel, but the entrepreneurs of the South Sea Company were determined that they could avoid the disaster of the Mississippi Scheme. 'Wise in their own conceit, they imagined they could avoid [John Law's] faults, carry on their schemes for ever, and stretch the cord of credit to its utmost tension, without causing it to snap asunder,' he says.

The times suit the people who profit from them. It hardly matters what the conditions were that produced the consensus that the South Sea Company was a good idea; what really matters is that a group of people thought it was a great idea, and they had enough credibility to enthuse the masses.

Taleb points out that in his history as a trader he has seen different styles of trader come and go, but that often they don't last, because from time to time the dynamics of the market will change. When they do, those who profited previously will often hold on to their ideas for too long without questioning them – and get wiped out.

Imagine a group of a hundred people all playing a game where a fair coin is tossed. They start with $1, and if they guess correctly, they double their money. They then stake everything on the second toss of the coin, and so on. If they lose, they lose everything.

After five flips there would most likely be three people who possessed $32 each, and ninety-seven who were broke and had gone home (more or less, but this is most likely). If you wanted to take advice on how to guess next time, who would you ask? You would, on average, do just as well to consult my pet turtle as to take advice from the 'winners'.

We invest survivors with insight which they may not deserve. In this example, it's clear that the successful ones can't tell us anything we don't know about coin flips; they got lucky. When you suspect a bubble, be careful who you talk to. Just because someone has made a wodge of cash from investing doesn't mean they know more than the people who didn't invest. They might, or they might just be the lucky survivors of an extraordinary random event.

HERE'S AN IDEA FOR YOU...

Don't build teams from your best performers who all think alike. It might pay to inject some dissent from someone with a different point of view (even if less successful so far).

20 THE BUBBLE THAT WASN'T

Was tulipomania a bubble or not? For some of the merchants, maybe, their losses were only on paper – and that's what caused the prices to go up.

Markets can boom if the risks aren't taken seriously. Mackay was in no doubt that tulipomania was an economic bubble that brought the economy of the Netherlands to its knees. 'Substantial merchants were reduced almost to beggary, and many a representative of a noble line saw the fortunes of his house ruined beyond redemption,' he says.

Maybe, but maybe not. Mackay's sources are thrown into doubt by modern research that shows the effects were not nearly as widespread as the chaos caused by the Mississippi Scheme or the South Sea Bubble.

DEFINING IDEA...

What most people don't seem to realise is that there is just as much money to be made out of the wreckage of a civilization as from the upbuilding of one.

~ MARGARET MITCHELL,
'GONE WITH THE WIND'

Maybe this is because in the headiest days of the bubble the contracts to buy were, in effect, futures contracts. There was a bulb season in the 1630s, and so the actual bulbs could only be bought and sold between June and September. That means that most of the contracts to buy and sell were promises: no money changed hands.

This wouldn't have saved the merchants who entered into silly contracts except for three other factors. There was a widespread belief that the contracts would never be enforced. In February 1637, as the mania was at its height, the Guild of Florists announced that all the contracts were, in effect, only options to buy. By paying a small penalty, the buyers didn't have to take the bulbs which they had contracted to buy. This had been widely anticipated, and it's a good example of how speculation booms in a market where the potential for profit (if the market stays good, simply take up your option) is much greater than the risk (if the market falls, pay your penalty).

The second is that the courts also refused to enforce the contracts that came out of the mania, considering them to be gambling debts. So the sellers were left, literally, holding the bulbs.

And finally, there was the plague. Other historians assert that as there was plague in Haarlem, where the trade was centred, it encouraged reckless behaviour from a group that might consider that at least one of the parties in a trade might soon be dead.

The tulipomania was probably, for most, more a collecting craze than a bubble. The downside was smaller than Mackay thought.

Similarly, we don't know if the current craze for billionaires to buy football clubs has created a price bubble among top players or just price inflation, but a player is currently an investment with potentially big profits (prices are going up, and if you buy a top player, maybe you'll win the league) and seemingly smaller risks (if you don't win the league, sell the player).

HERE'S AN IDEA FOR YOU...

When a deal's not definite, always take into account the risk to you and to your counterparty of it collapsing. It may be small for them – in which case, try making their commitment more tangible, either in money, time or reputation.

21 WHAT DON'T YOU KNOW?

Bubbles and panics are often created when one side of the deal knows something the other doesn't.

Behaviour such as drowning someone because she might be a witch or paying a fortune for a tulip would be described by a behavioural economist as 'sub-optimal'. Thanks to the research of modern economists, we can now begin to understand some of the reasons why we behave oddly.

'People who had been absent from Holland, and whose chance it was to return when this folly was at its maximum, were sometimes led into awkward dilemmas by their ignorance,' Mackay notes of the tulip mania. He goes on to tell a not-very-credible anecdote of someone eating an expensive bulb, thinking it was an onion, but that's not the point.

As Economics Nobel Prize winner Joseph Stiglitz and others have pointed out, asymmetrical information creates problems in business. In any deal, if both sides are well-informed about the product and the market, the prices can be fairly set by negotiation. If one side knows more than the other, those prices get skewed. Imagine, for example, a second-hand-car salesman.

In our bubbles, the asymmetries were everywhere. In the Mississippi Scheme, the people who rushed to buy the stock at the beginning didn't know that the government would keep on issuing more of it, and they didn't know the truth about the Mississippi. The South Sea Bubble and the other joint stock companies that accompanied it, were posited on sketchy information. In both those circumstances, people relied too much on the behaviour of others, and we can do exactly the same.

Asymmetries are still with us today. People invested in merchant banks because they had little conception of how exposed those banks were to bad loans – and that's because the complex derivatives that parcelled up those bad loans were impossible to unravel. Even a simple job interview uncovers an asymmetry: if you're interviewing someone, and your ad asked for a happy person, then everyone will act happy at the interview. They will all claim to be happy all the time and even insert a few lines about happiness into their CVs, because they think that they will improve their prospects of getting a job by doing so.

Businesses are also ruined by asymmetries. If, for example, we hear that a company is selling some substandard product, then the price of the products or the demand for them will usually decline, because we will be unwilling to commit to products that might turn out to be substandard. Hence, after the problems of Terminal 5 at Heathrow, BA took to running advertising showing the previous days' passengers having a pleasant trip. We only had the information that Terminal 5 was a nightmare from press reports at the shambolic opening.

HERE'S AN IDEA FOR YOU...

The internet corrects asymmetries efficiently. One example is giving complete price transparency and encouraging your customers to search other sites for a better deal. You could also show feedback from other customers. If you have confidence in what you do, transparency is your friend. It will drive prices or volumes up.

22 FOREVER BLOWING BUBBLES

How do you spot a bubble? It's hard at the time, but easier with hindsight.

And so I reach the end of my musings on the first three chapters of *Extraordinary Popular Delusions*. Don't worry, there's plenty more to follow. It gets weirder.

DEFINING IDEA...

Speculation is only a word covering the making of money out of the manipulation of prices, instead of supplying goods and services.
~ HENRY FORD

But that's basically the end of the chapters on economic bubbles, chapters that could have been written yesterday, last week or fifty years ago. Bubbles have proved to be a consistent feature of the economic landscape. 'In times of great commercial prosperity there has been a tendency to over-speculation on several occasions since then,' wrote Mackay, at the end of his history of the South Sea Bubble. He published just too early for the railway mania of 1845, and died before bubbles like the craze to build hotels in Florida, collect Beanie Babies and cabbage patch dolls, the Asian crisis in the late 1990s or the dot-com boom. In early 2008 there was even a short-lived bubble on eBay as people competed to bid for cornflakes shaped like US states. I'm not making this up. The winners must be feeling pretty foolish.

All these had the classic tell-tale signs of bubbles. But how do we spot a bubble?

Economists are by no means united in how to define a bubble (that makes sense; they're still debating how to define economics), but for the rest of us there are a few rules. A bubble divorces the value that you pay for something from its 'intrinsic' value. Every price seems too low, because the price keeps going up. So more people buy, which pushes the price up further.

Here's the catch: we rarely spot bubbles as they occur. We can often identify them with hindsight, but that's not a lot of use if you're investing. It takes a strong stomach, when a price keeps rising, to hold fast to your belief that it was fairly priced at half its current price. The idea of intrinsic pricing tends to get revised as experts clamour to tell us that the 'old rules' no longer apply. Here's an example. Before the dot-com boom, intrinsic measures of value were usually based on earnings. But dot-com companies had little or no earnings, so we simply found new measures of value – for a while.

What causes a bubble? It appears they're unavoidable. They constantly recur even among experts investing in markets where intrinsic value is relatively easy to assess. Groupthink, greed and a popular theory that bigger and bigger fools buy at higher prices – until the pool of fools is exhausted – could all be the cause. But it's probably true to say that the lesson of Mackay's bubbles is that all three contribute, and continue to contribute, in exactly the same way today as they did 400 years ago.

Look out for bubbles. Avoid them if you can. But most of us, some time, are going to get fooled.

HERE'S AN IDEA FOR YOU...

The only way to avoid taking heavy losses from a bubble bursting in your investments is to spread your portfolio, and to have a strict exit strategy: define a maximum loss you will take before getting out.

23 TURNING WASTED TIME INTO GOLD

The search for the philosopher's stone and the secret of transmuting metals was one of the great wastes of talent in history – or was it?

Many, many pages of Mackay's book are given to an exhaustive list of mini-biographies of every major figure in the search for the secret of how to make lead into gold and the quest for the philosopher's stone which gives eternal life.

DEFINING IDEA...
Destiny is something we've invented because we can't stand the fact that everything that happens is accidental.
~ MEG RYAN, 'IN SLEEPLESS IN SEATTLE'

'Three causes especially have excited the discontent of mankind,' Mackay points out, 'death, toil and ignorance of the future.' From this condition came the alchemists. Many people would argue that there wasn't any real difference between chemistry and the research into alchemy until the eighteenth century.

The first of the great alchemists (if we discount Noah, who was assumed to be an adept, having fathered children at the age of 500) is now known as Geber. Geber's alchemical experiments weren't a complete failure. Just the alchemy bit was, which is a recurring theme in alchemy.

Thought to have lived around AD 730, his real name was Abou Moussah Djafar. He had a lot to say about alchemy: he wrote more than 500 works on it, so it's surprising that he had any time to do the actual experiments.

His theory was that all metals were diseased, except gold, so his research was like finding a cure.

This he didn't do. But: 'He stumbled upon discoveries that he did not seek, and science is indebted to him for the first mention of corrosive sublimate, the red oxide of mercury, nitric acid and the nitrate of silver.' This is, we should recall, at a time when many of the inhabitants of Western Europe were barely past the stage of covering themselves in woad for fun.

While we can laugh at the alchemists now, and we shall, it's worth remembering that these grand passions can have unexpected benefits. Time and again, the alchemists who followed Geber were driven to experiment, to exchange knowledge and books, and to travel to try and find information about the principles of what we now know as chemistry. The central project was a failure, but the obsession of making gold gave us knowledge – and scientists – that otherwise would have been lost.

Mackay didn't know that one of the greatest scientists, Sir Isaac Newton, was a keen alchemist. Newton kept his alchemical work a secret (strictly speaking it was illegal, and anyway if he found the secret he wasn't telling everyone), but he took it as seriously as his other crazy ideas such as gravity and calculus.

Now, you might think the space programme has been a waste. But spin-offs include better golf ball design, the self-righting inflatable boat – and a few other things like improved cancer detection, better weather forecasting and cheaper water purification systems. Space scientists don't yet have the secret of eternal life though – or, if they do, they're not telling – like Newton.

HERE'S AN IDEA FOR YOU...

Look out for spin-offs and side benefits; be open-minded. Companies like Google formally give their engineers time to work on their own ideas, some of which are turned into products.

24 RIPLEY'S BELIEVE IT OR NOT

Clever people may believe some pretty barmy stuff. When they do, too many of us believe them for too long – and they can even fool themselves.

One of the most interesting of the alchemists Mackay discusses (though not notably more successful than any of the others) was George Ripley, canon of Bridlington and favourite of Pope Innocent VIII. Ripley was heir to a tradition of ecclesiastical would-be alchemists; Henry IV had granted letters patent to four of them, probably figuring that if they succeeded he wanted a piece of the action, and if they failed, he'd lost nothing. Why priests? Because, Mackay decides, they were adept at turning water into wine, so base metal into gold couldn't be much more difficult.

Henry's successor Edward IV was the lucky dedicatee of Ripley's great work of 1477, *The Compound of Alchemy; or, the 12 Gates Leading to the Discovery of the Philosopher's Stone*. The twelve gates include calcination, separation and putrefaction, 'to which one might have added botheration, the most important process of all,' adds Mackay.

Later in life Ripley retired to Boston in Lincolnshire, where he obviously had some time on his hands and a talent for fiction. He pumped out a staggering twenty-five books about alchemy. And then, before he died, '… he seems to have acknowledged that he spent his life in this vain study, and requested that all men, when they met with any of his books, would burn them … as they had been written purely from his opinion'.

In short, he made them up. When he tried out his twelve -ations, they didn't work.

Denial is a powerful force. Here's an example. Few adults can even remember the time that the US auto industry was the world leader. For many years Japanese companies have been grabbing US market share by building small, economical cars – the sort of vehicles that GM, Ford and Chrysler said that Americans didn't want.

Recently, with GM and Ford shares in the gutter and Chrysler in private ownership, and quarterly losses in the billions of dollars, the CEOs of Ford and GM at least have reformed their ways. These companies weren't run by stupid people; quite the opposite. But in 600 years not much has changed. When we want to believe something, and someone we respect has a plausible story, it reinforces our belief that they must be right. Sometimes it reinforces their own belief too, even beyond what the evidence of their own eyes shows them to be true.

Ripley couldn't make iron into gold. Detroit's CEOs couldn't make trucks into profit. Deathbed conversions are all very well – but something a little earlier would help more people.

HERE'S AN IDEA FOR YOU...

In the office or at home, don't wait too long to 'fess up to the things that, deep down inside, you no longer believe. You might be surprised to find who agrees with you when you give them the confidence to say something.

25 THE NEED TO BELIEVE

Sometimes a relatively simple trick can deceive us – because we want to believe.

DEFINING IDEA...

Frank Abagnale: Brenda, I don't want to lie to you anymore. All right? I'm not a doctor. I never went to medical school. I'm not a lawyer, or a Harvard graduate or a Lutheran. Brenda, I ran away from home a year and a half ago when I was 16. Brenda Strong: Frank? You're not a Lutheran?

– FROM 'CATCH ME IF YOU CAN'

The people that Mackay calls the 'inferior' alchemists were no less successful in real terms than the rest of them. Many were very successful precisely because they took the simple short cut to success: they cheated. 'The trick to which they oftenest had recourse, was to use a double bottomed crucible, the under surface being iron or copper, and the upper one of wax, painted to resemble the same metal. Between the two they placed as much gold or silver dust as was necessary for their purpose,' he explains. When the crucible was heated, it never failed to produce precious metal, no matter what else went into it. Another handy trick was to use a hollow rod, which had been filled with gold dust and stoppered with wax at one end, to stir the concoction in the crucible. Their rewards were, according to Mackay, '…entrances into royal households, maintenance at the public expense, and gifts from ambitious potentates, too greedy after the gold they so easily promised'.

A confidence trick, contrary to popular belief, isn't about the confidence of the trickster. It is founded in our confidence in the person who is bilking us. Mackay must have known of one of the greatest con men of all, Gregor Macgregor, who turned up in London in 1820 claiming to be the cazique of Poyais, a nation in South America. He sold land in Poyais and chartered a ship for settlers, who enthusiastically bought the Poyais dollars that he had printed. Then, when their ship landed in South America, they were informed that there was no such place as Poyais by local people. Most of the travellers perished of disease, but most of those who survived believed that Macgregor was the victim, not the perpetrator, of the con. That's real confidence.

Perhaps the best recent example of the confidence man is Gert Postel, who despite being trained only as a postman successfully worked as a medical doctor in Germany during the 1980s and 1990s. He was recognised when working as a psychiatrist in 1997, just before his appointment to a professorship as chief of medicine at Saxony's hospital for psychiatry and neurology.

There are mercifully few big-time confidence men active today. But the small-time con men flourish. You might be one yourself, or be a victim of one. When the Risk Advisory Group screened 3700 CVs in an experiment in 2006, half of the CVs they looked at contained lies – and one in five contained a serious lie. We all want to believe the people who work for us are as talented and experienced as they say they are. Likely as not, they aren't.

HERE'S AN IDEA FOR YOU...

When you recruit, do the simplest checking on the CVs you are presented with – for example, universities will tell you about qualifications, and previous employers might confirm job titles. It may save you from disaster.

26 THE BIG SHILL

Con men need help from accomplices who exploit our desire to believe them.

The Count de St Germain was considered in his day to be a mysterious and powerful man, one who had great influence in the court of Louis XV. 'He pretended to have discovered the elixir of life,' writes Mackay, 'by means of which he could make anyone live for centuries.' To make this seem more credible he let it be known that he was no spring chicken: he was, he told his many admirers, more than 2000 years old.

To reinforce this image, the Count was never at a loss to describe anyone from history that he might have met. His skill as a storyteller was used to turn the tables on his (quite reasonable) critics, who would often ask him to describe some illustrious person who was long dead. He admitted to his closest friends (for example, Madame de Pompadour), that really this was simply a lucrative joke. 'I have an excellent memory... and have read the history of France with great care,' he told her.

But one of his most convincing accomplices was his servant. 'The fellow, who was not without ability, generally corroborated him in a most amusing manner,' reports Mackay. One time when the Count was telling the story of his friendship with Richard I of England, he wasn't believed. He turned round to ask his servant if his account was true. 'I really cannot say,' the servant replied, 'you forget, sir, I have only been 500 years in your service.'

This servant was a fine example of the con man's essential helper, the shill. A shill's job is to appear to be either neutral or on the side of the mark (the person being conned), but in reality he is working to help the con. Most of us will have been tempted in the past by the shell game, or find the lady. In the shell game, a small ball is placed under one of three cups. The con man shuffles the cups, taking care to give you a fleeting glimpse of the location of the ball. You hesitate, at which point someone leaps in, puts their money down, and wins the bet. They encourage you to get involved. You see the obvious location of the ball on the next turn, bet – and lose.

The shill succeeds because he or she reinforces what you want to believe – even if, logically, you know it's too good to be true.

What you don't know is that you are the only person in the crowd who isn't part of the scam. Before you can win your money back, someone will claim to spot the police arriving, and the whole operation suddenly packs up and disappears, but with your cash.

HERE'S AN IDEA FOR YOU...

One of the most irritating ways you will encounter shills today is in any bid process. Fake bidders are used to raise a price, and not just on eBay. Resist competing in any auction where someone seems too enthusiastic to raise a price. It's not that they know something you don't. They're often shills.

27 PURE QUACKERY

The world is full of charlatans, quacks and well-meaning fools who exploit our willingness to believe. They're just as powerful as ever.

When alchemy fell into disrepute 'a new delusion, based on the power of imagination, suddenly arose', as Mackay puts it in his chapter on magnetisers.

DEFINING IDEA...

Homoeopathy is insignificant as an art of healing, but of great value as criticism on the medical practice of the time.
~ RALPH WALDO EMERSON

The magnetisers indulged in an early form of pseudo-science. The alchemist Paracelsus decided that magnets could suck disease out of people and into the ground. This knowledge – sorry, I mean 'childish fantasy' – spread, until all over the world quacks were making people with perfectly respectable tumours swallow iron filings so that the magnet could suck the cancer out of the body with the metal.

By the middle of the seventeenth century the idea had spread – to the extent that many people believed that if someone had been injured by a sword it was sufficient to magnetise the sword to cure the injury. There's still a large industry dedicated to the effects of magnetic wotsits for healing this and that. There's not a shred of reliable evidence that it actually works, so don't try the sword thing with your mates as a party trick.

The magnetisers spread the miraculous tales of their craft using the type of evidence humans prefer: anecdotal stories of people we've never met. For example, the fine tale of Mr James Howell, whose hand was almost severed in the reign of King James when he tried to stop his friends from duelling, as related by Mackay. When Sir Kenelm Digby got involved, he soaked a bloody garter in a magnetised fluid, dried the garter in front of the fire, and managed to cure Mr Howell's hand in six days. Not bad going, considering Howell wasn't even in the same room as the garter.

Quacks couldn't get away with this sort of thing today. Or could they? Homeopathy, used by 2% of the British public and on offer in five NHS hospitals, is based on the idea that you dilute a quantity of a substance like sulphur repeatedly, and then use it to cure common ailments. The dilution is extreme: a 30C solution will have one molecule of the 'active' ingredient in ten (to the power of) sixty molecules of water: you would need to take an amazing two billion pills to consume one molecule of the active substance. A common flu remedy has a ratio of 1:10 (to the power of) 400 molecules of duck liver. A 12C solution – many millions of times more concentrated than that – is equivalent to adding a pinch of salt to the Atlantic.

There's no reliable evidence that these work beyond the effect of a placebo, except that the descendents of Sir Kenelm tell us they do, and tell stories of people we don't know. Where can you get them? Try your local chemist. We're really no smarter than people were in the past. Today our quack medicines just have better packaging.

HERE'S AN IDEA FOR YOU...

If someone offers you a case study or a testimonial as proof that their idea works, have a policy of always following it up and speaking to the person cited yourself.

28 NOT IN THE STARS

We can't control everything, but that doesn't mean we have to believe any fool who claims that the alignment of planets has the answer.

DEFINING IDEA...

I don't believe in astrology; I'm a Sagittarius and we're sceptical.

~ ARTHUR C. CLARKE

In 1736 a prophecy that the world would be destroyed encouraged Londoners to head for Islington and Hampstead, so that they could view the destruction of London (why they thought they would escape isn't recorded). In Leeds, in 1806, a hen caused panic by laying eggs with 'Christ is coming' written on them. It turned out, on further inspection, that the eggs had already been laid once, after which the owner had written on them and popped them back in the aforesaid chicken to be laid a second time.

Why were so many people prepared to believe in this twaddle? As Mackay points out, the essential ingredient in all this was a widespread 'belief in fatalism' – the illusion that the future has been somehow determined, and we just have to look for clues as to how it will work out.

We're not so different today, but instead of the end of the world we often want to find out about whether we should be doing business deals. If you consult the website of 'Magi Helena', you'll see that she claims that several business leaders consult her regularly to find out such gems as: 'ONLY A DOZEN OR SO OF THE DAYS IN ANY YEAR CAN BE SUCCESSFUL INCORPORATION, PARTNERSHIP, OR PRODUCT RELEASE DATES – and only a handful of those would bring Super-Success both in a particular industry AND for a particular owner/majority stockholder or for particular partners.' Her evidence?

Well, Microsoft, Dell, Harley-Davidson, General Electric, Oracle, Amgen and Apple were all incorporated on super-success days, apparently, and 'The most profitable website in the world, eBay, bought their domain name on 8/4/1995, a day which had 3 Golden super aspects, 10 Silver super aspects, and specific patterns supporting Super-Success in bringing people together for buying and selling on the internet.' By contrast, AOL/Time-Warner merged on a ' triple Financial Heartbreak day' and 'Enron's re-incorporation on July 17, 1996, had 0 Golden or Silver aspects, a Financial Heartbreak aspect, and a pattern indicating it would be a short-lived entity'.

Whether or not Magi Helena really has any business clients, this type of rubbish is dangerous the minute you let it influence you, because it encourages you to believe that the forces out of your control are planetary. Yes, there are some factors you can't influence – but the minute you are at all fatalistic about them, you are like a rabbit trapped in the headlights. Look closer to home for weaknesses, and deal with them. Unless, of course, you're a Pisces, in which case you will prefer to sit back and let things happen.

HERE'S AN IDEA FOR YOU...

Prophecy is a dangerous business – some things are likely, some are unlikely. The effects of some unlikely things might be devastating. But nothing is pre-ordained. Establish a group to look at long-term risks, five or ten years into the future. Just don't include an astrologer in it..

29 UNDER A SPELL

Even for people who don't understand how they do it, our minds are surprisingly easy to control.

We've forgotten the magnetisers today, but in Mackay's time they were still quite the rage. It was less than a hundred years since Mesmer, celebrated physician, entrepreneur and patron of the young Mozart, had thrilled Paris with his concept of 'Animal Magnetism', designed to heal what the modern physicians would call 'just about anything'.

Mesmer flirted with the early theory of the magnetisers – the one idea that swallowing iron filings and having a magnet pointed at you did any good at all. But he soon decided that the attribute which cured people was his own 'magnetism'.

DEFINING IDEA...

We are all in a post-hypnotic trance induced in early infancy.

~ R. D. LAING

His treatment involved sitting his patients with him, vigorously stroking them, fixing them with his eyes, and that's about it – often for whole roomfuls of people. Mackay quotes a physician of the time: 'In the middle of the room is placed a vessel of about a foot and a half high which is called here a "baquet". It is so large that twenty people can easily sit round it ... there are holes pierced corresponding to the number of persons who are to surround it; into these holes are introduced iron rods, bent at right angles outwards...' and so on. The whole contraption reliably effected convulsions in those who dared to sit around it. Afterwards, they usually pronounced themselves miraculously cured.

It all ended with a bit of a whimper for Mesmer, as belief in his barmy methods gradually drained away. But he left two legacies for us. One is the word 'mesmerised', of course, for someone who is under the spell of someone or something. And as Mackay was writing, another physician was using Mesmer's writings to help develop a new therapeutic process, called 'hypnotism'.

It's still not obvious how hypnosis works, but experiments which have been completed show that Mesmer was on to something far more important than he could have realised. The fact that our brains are open to suggestion, and that some people unconsciously desire to hand over their critical faculty to another person, is now accepted in science. The brain function of a hypnotised person who believes he or she is seeing or experiencing something is identical to someone who actually is seeing or experiencing it. Hypnosis, used wisely, can help healing and psychological problems, and encourage us to do better.

Mesmer wasn't the first person to profit by the power of suggestion; healers had been doing it for centuries without realising it. He wasn't even the first hypnotist, as there's plenty of evidence for it in early religion, for example. But he was the first person to try to analyse the power for what it was.

In the end, it didn't matter whether his 'baquet' worked or not. But by using it to put his subjects under his power, he helped many of them – almost without realising it.

HERE'S AN IDEA FOR YOU...

You can easily mesmerise yourself, when you're absorbed in a book, for instance. People such as sports psychologists or clinical hypnotists can teach you how to harness this ability to improve concentration and confidence, or target a goal. Athletes use it, and so do a surprising number of successful executives.

30 IT'S A SIGN

Divination uses inanimate objects to help us believe in things that we want to hear. It's easy to confuse science with mumbo-jumbo if we just focus on the result.

'There are thousands and tens of thousands of humble families in which the good-wife, and even the good-man, resort to the grounds at the bottom of their teacups, to know whether the next harvest will be abundant,' complains Mackay in part of his chapter on the batty world of divination.

For fans of divination, he helpfully lists a number of different techniques, including omphelomancy, the art of telling the future using the navel; gastromancy, by the sounds of the stomach; ceromancy, by the melting of wax; axinomancy, by saws; koskinomancy, by sieves; and, of course, tyromancy, the art of seeing the future in cheese.

Half the time today we make fun of the people who predict the future (onomancy, the art of prediction by using the letters of your name, has been replaced by jokes about how to create your stripper name). The other half of the time, of course, we're just as much in thrall to modern-day diviners.

One of the most staggering modern-day examples is water divining, known as dowsing; the experts use a Y-shaped rod or similar device to find hidden water. How harmless is this? Well, mostly. But as with much of this mumbo-jumbo, the problem is often the indirect harm that it causes.

Look at Jersey, an island that doesn't have enough water. Using desalination to provide water costs seventy times as much as storing it in a reservoir. The alternative is to enforce restrictions on water use – not a popular policy.

Actually there's one more alternative: the local water diviners are convinced that Jersey's water is replenished by an underground stream from France. The government's geologists have surveyed Jersey, and decided that this is almost impossible. But many of Jersey's most senior politicians prefer to believe the diviners, and are convinced that the underground streams exist. The Jersey government drilled two boreholes at the spots that the diviners claimed would uncover the underground streams. When they took water out of the ground and tested it, it was identical to Jersey rainwater, not to the water which would have come under the sea from France. So far, there's been no evidence to support the diviners' case. Meanwhile Jersey doesn't get the water regulations it needs.

This is the problem with using inanimate objects to divine things with which they have no connection. As long as they tell us something we really want to hear, we're likely to assign some credibility to that point of view above more reliable, but more negative, scientific results. The audience for Jersey's diviners wants to hear that everything will be fine – and I note that no diviner has yet gone to Jersey and concluded that there is no underground stream.

HERE'S AN IDEA FOR YOU...

We like to hear good news, so sometimes we trust unreliable sources. Don't make decisions based on what fits your preconceptions; look at the facts and the statistical basis first.

31 FUTURE IMPERFECT

Nostradamus: mostly wrong, not very useful – like most research...

DEFINING IDEA...

Near the harbours, and within two cities,

There will be two catastrophes such as never before seen...

~ NOSTRADAMUS, 'PRECISELY' PREDICTING THE ATOM BOMB. OR NOT.

Fortune tellers were as popular in Mackay's time as today, and they made a great deal of money or fame out of their 'success'. Mackay lists several of them, notably Nostradamus – whose weird and obscure stanzas are always brought up after something dramatic happens. The prophecies are 'to the full as obscure as the oracles of old,' Mackay says. 'They take so great a latitude, both as to time and space, that they are almost sure to be fulfilled somewhere or other.'

Nostradamus' fans would tell us that he predicted the rise of Hitler, the death of Princess Diana, the Challenger Space Shuttle disaster, the Great Fire of London and 9/11. The problem is that even when it's not a mistranslation or a fabrication, Nostradamus is completely useless before the event. On 10 September 2001 no one said, 'I've been reading this quatrain and we need to do something about airline security' or, in 1997, 'Having looked at these prophecies we had better tell Princess Diana to wear her seat belt.'

Nevertheless the ability to predict the future is enormously lucrative today, for everyone from stock-market analysts to weather forecasters.

The success of Nostradamus can teach us about how we could usefully predict the future. The first is that he was deliberately vague. Often financial forecasts will predict that GDP growth in a country four years from now will be 4.3%, for example. This is useless as a planning tool; it's a result of hundreds of calculations, all with small room for error. What matters is a range of outcomes (say, 3–5.5% with 60% confidence, others less likely, plus a tiny chance that something disastrous will happen). Once you know the range, you can have a strategy for each outcome.

Nostradamus also copied a lot of his prophecies – but it's no good using research because 'it has been right in the past'. Every idiot is right sooner or later. You need to make an argument that the method is sound, not the result.

Nostradamus also liked to concentrate on unexpected major events. When you're making strategy, these are by definition hard to predict – but disruptive events (the growth of the internet is a 'good' example, the credit crunch a 'bad' one) can have far more effect on long-term planning than all the carefully shaded possibilities of your risk analysis. Without a strategy to deal with rare events you simply don't have a strategy.

On the evening of 1 July 1566, Nostradamus was very sick. He said to his servant that 'you will not find me alive' the next morning, abandoning his usual vagueness. For the first – and last – time he made a specific prediction and got it right.

HERE'S AN IDEA FOR YOU...

When you're doing your planning, allow for what the philosopher David Hume first called 'Black Swan' events – very rare ones, but events that completely change our view of the world. Don't plan only for the obvious, because eventually a rare and disruptive event will occur.

32 SUGAR PILLS

A placebo doesn't have any medical effect, but that doesn't make it bad.

'The wonderful influence of imagination in the cure of diseases is well known,' Mackay writes to introduce his chapter on the magnetisers. 'A pill made of bread, if taken with sufficient faith, will operate a cure better than all the drugs in pharmacopoeia.'

Mackay calls the magnetisers 'a new delusion'; but often they made people believe they were being healed. This placebo effect was already well known. It means that when we are given a medicine which has no reason in science to help us, we sometimes feel better (or even recover). It's natural that we attribute the healing power to whatever we took or whatever we did.

DEFINING IDEA...

Sugar pills are the future, if only there was a way to give them with integrity, and a straight face.

~ DR BEN GOLDACRE,
AUTHOR OF 'BAD SCIENCE'

The placebo effect was undoubtedly exploited by the magnetisers. But, like many of the madnesses that Mackay points out, we're still doing it today. All sorts of misapplied pharmaceutical remedies – antibiotics for viral illnesses like colds, or cough mixture for, er, coughs, or most antidepressants – have been found to have little or no medical effect. If we feel better, we often attribute it to the thing we did that was intended to make us feel better, even if we would have felt better anyway.

There are two essential features of a placebo. The first is that it has to be a positive intervention. We prefer doctors who prescribe something over those who tell us to go home and go to bed for a few days. We also need to believe that what they prescribe will work before we take it.

Recent research shows that a placebo's action can be medically measurable. An example is research done on pain relief. Subjects given a placebo reported a reduction in pain. When they were given a drug that blocked opiates (without being informed), the pain returned. The conclusion was that the belief that they were taking a pain killer stimulated the brain to release the body's own opiates. The pain relief was 'real'.

Leadership has a well-established placebo effect. One example is healing using the power of prayer, where scientific evidence shows no link. But many people report that being prayed for lessens their pain.

There are, however, limits. Many years ago, I was employed as a cameraman at a religious rock festival. The warm up act was a faith healer, who promised that if the audience prayed hard enough, a small boy in a wheelchair would be able to walk again. 'Keep your camera on him,' the director told me, 'it won't work, but I don't want to be the director that missed a miracle.'

HERE'S AN IDEA FOR YOU...

The important part of a placebo is that people believe in it. Any project that people believe in has a much better chance of success — which is why, whenever you're attempting to change something, you need to appoint a champion for your project, someone credible who will 'sell' it.

33 HAIR TODAY

Looking like the boss makes you feel good, but you're an individual.

DEFINING IDEA...

Wisdom is in the head and not in the beard.

– SWEDISH PROVERB

In a short yet incident-packed chapter that takes us from the shaving customs of Alexander the Great through the Normans, the royalty of Europe, the Crusaders and finally to Peter the Great, Mackay reminds us of the influence of politics on how men wear their hair – long or short (think Roundheads and Cavaliers), shaven or unshaven, moustaches or goatees.

The theme that runs through the chapter is that whether we want to look like the leader, or the leader tells us how to look, conforming is one of the simplest ways to advertise our loyalty.

Here are a couple of examples. In the reign of Henri IV of France, all his courtiers sported beards, like Henri himself. After he died, his successor was too young to have a beard. And so the men of the court had to shave if they knew what was good for them. In Russia, Peter the Great decided to ape the fashion of Europe, and force his male subjects to shave their beloved beards. They didn't much like it, but a fine of 100 roubles for those who didn't shave was an incentive.

Today we don't tend to take instruction from our rulers about how to shave or cut our hair (outside of some religious states, and some of the barmier dictatorships). Often though, we're still involved in an exercise of copy-your-leader.

In the US, the spirit of Abraham Lincoln has not lived on: clean-shavenness is associated with trust. Surveys show that politicians with beards poll on average 5% less than clean-shaven opponents. The British Labour party also suggested to Frank Dobson, when he stood for mayor of London, that he should shave off his beard. He didn't, and he lost.

One of the most interesting experiences I had of copy-your-leader was the tendency in the late 1980s and early 1990s for male employees of Sir Alan Sugar (when he was chief executive of Amstrad) to sport small, clipped beards. It started with his number two Malcolm Miller, but any number of product managers and marketing executives sported the same look – and the same bulldog style that suited the beard so well. There wasn't a formal rule that said they had to have beards, but the desire to fit in with the boss can be just as strong.

It doesn't stop with beards and haircuts. One magazine that I worked for had a memorably abusive culture of management by shouting. It was shocking to see pleasant, unassuming recruits turn into yelling monsters almost overnight. Luckily, when they left, most of them changed back. Compared to that, growing a beard to fit in doesn't seem like such a bad choice.

HERE'S AN IDEA FOR YOU...

Look around you at work. Who do you try to look like? Tomorrow, dress to reflect your own personality. Get your hair cut, but don't take a picture of a celebrity with you for the stylist to copy. That's exactly what you shouldn't do.

34 AN ORDINARY BLOKE

Peter the Hermit helped to start two centuries of slaughter by using his man-of-the-people image to promote a needless war.

What started the Crusades? There's never one cause, but one of the figures who Mackay singles out is the now almost forgotten Peter the Hermit.

DEFINING IDEA...

The secret of the demagogue is to make himself as stupid as his audience so that they believe they are as clever as he.

~ KARL KRAUS, AUSTRIAN WRITER AND SATIRIST

Peter was 'exactly suited to the age… the people so highly reverenced him that they plucked hairs from the mane of his mule,' he says. Peter, given the mission to preach by Pope Urban II, went through France, Germany and Italy exciting the passions of the whole of a continent, dressed in simple clothes and hardly stopping to rest. His speeches aren't recorded, but they convinced the masses to sell their possessions and give up everything, and follow him to an unknown fate. By the time that the Pope addressed a fervent crowd in Clermont in 1095, all eyes were on Peter, 'humbler in rank, but more important in the world's eye'.

Peter later proved to be an incompetent leader, especially compared to the experienced warmongers who came later, as his huge army of crusaders pillaged their way through Bulgaria and ripped the lead off the church roofs in Constantinople. History doesn't record exactly where he ended up. It's fair to say that he was not 'exactly suited to the age' for a long time. Nevertheless, he had achieved his purpose.

What makes a demagogue like Peter successful? In presenting himself as a man of the people who had witnessed the barbarity that the Muslims wrought, and demonising a culture that – at the time – was arguably more advanced and sophisticated than European feudalism, he successfully appealed to our tendency to go for emotion over logic. People trusted him because he wasn't like the remote, privileged leaders they scarcely knew. His clothes and attitude, and his claim to be born without privilege, made him an effective man of the people at the same time.

The skill of the demagogue has been central to many destructive mass movements since. We now understand much more about how people like Peter do their work: offering half-truths (the barbarity of the Muslims), false dilemmas (if Jerusalem wasn't retaken, Christianity would be extinguished), demonisation and cloaking himself in the authority of the Pope.

We see the same behaviour in every small-time rabble-rouser: a man (it's usually a man) who's one of us but with a higher calling, who can successfully dehumanise the opposition and can appeal to our emotions by creating a sense of imminent danger.

There's a danger in our world that the Internet, usually promoted as an antidote to the demagogues, can instead promote them by giving them a platform. It's not true that everyone has a right to broadcast their opinion if that opinion is factually wrong and likely to have destructive consequences. Sadly, if Peter the Hermit were alive today, he'd probably be blogging.

HERE'S AN IDEA FOR YOU...

Understanding people who disagree with you means listening to them, which means meeting them in person. Debates conducted at arm's length or on email can lead to each side demonising the other. Organise a meeting instead.

35 TELLING TALES

Just because everyone believes something, it's not necessarily the truth.

Whether you're a witch or the witness to a miracle depends on whose interests you're serving. I'm not talking about whether you're in league with the Devil or a servant of God here – I'm more interested in whose earthly power you're in touch with.

DEFINING IDEA...

What a man believes upon grossly insufficient evidence is an index into his desires.

– BERTRAND RUSSELL

The torturers of accused witches, working on behalf of religious leaders, kings and other politicians on the make, managed to extract some quite detailed confessions. Indeed, as Mackay points out more than once, these confessions were often strikingly alike, almost as if they had been written out first to suit the aims of the accuser.

The siege of Antioch during the first Crusade also gave rise to one of the most exciting yet completely made up visions in the history of political religion. The crusaders, who had got into the city but were stuck outside the citadel, weren't getting anywhere. Suddenly, a poor priest called Peter Balthelemy showed up at the tent of Count Raymond of Toulouse, claiming that in a dream St Andrew had taken him to the church of St Peter in Antioch, then being used as a mosque, and had shown him that the spear which pierced the side of Christ was buried beneath the floor.

When the knowledge of this wonderful happening was spread around, it was decided to dig for this spear. 'The Count of Toulouse who, in all probability, concocted this precious tale with the priest' (Mackay) led the dig. After some time, Peter leapt into the hole, and miraculously located the spear which the Count had no doubt buried earlier, and this served to unite and reinvigorate the army in its campaign.

The power of myth exists not in its truth or falsity, but in our willingness to believe. and that belief exists because it taps into a deep-seated emotional need: for security, for validation, for a sense of purpose.

Today those narratives are often created or adapted for the political and commercial world. Marketing has taken the elements of these narratives, and uses them to connect with our need for popularity, success and wealth. If we don't purchase consumer goods, we will be social outcasts. If we don't have identity cards, we will be overrun by criminal foreigners. If we dress in fashion, people will find our personality attractive. Disentangling myth from reality is as hard as it was when Peter jumped out of a hole in a church with a perfectly ordinary spear and claimed, Blues-Brothers style, that he was on a mission from God – when really he was on a mission from his boss.

HERE'S AN IDEA FOR YOU...

We rarely test assumptions that we 'know' to be true. 'Gut feeling' helps solve simple problems, but the complex decisions we often have to make in business need reliable statistical data. Demand proof in meetings, not opinions.

36 COUNT THE COST

Reaching your goal sometimes comes at an unacceptably high cost for the people around you.

'The most extraordinary instance upon record of the extent to which popular enthusiasm can be carried,' is Mackay's conclusion on the Crusades. Nowadays we're a bit vague on exactly what the crusaders were doing, when they did it and how successful they were, so it's instructive to read his exhaustive and bloody review of the Crusades, one by one.

Here are some facts that might surprise you.

For 200 years before the First Crusade, Christian pilgrims had visited Palestine without running into any opposition; some had been killed, but generally the inhabitants of Jerusalem knew that pilgrims were good for business.

The First Crusade in 1096 was marked by robbery, pillage and destruction of the countries through which it marched – notably Hungary, which was, over the years, seen as a sort of free refuelling station for millions of crusaders. The crusaders under 'Walter the Pennyless' were, Mackay tells us, 'destructive as a plague of locusts'.

One of the armies of the First Crusade was fanatically committed to slaughtering Jews, and 'so dreadful was the cruelty of their tormentors, that great numbers of Jews committed self-destruction to avoid falling into their hands'. Jews and Muslims fought together against the crusaders who were invading their country.

It was routine to massacre the civilian population after a battle. Crusaders are recorded to have committed cannibalism after the siege of Maarat in 1098.

How many Crusades to Palestine were there? Three? Four? In a little under 200 years, there were no less than nine. Millions died, and more were impoverished by the taxes that had to be raised to organise the Crusades and arm the soldiers. The result was that Palestine was under Western rule for about a hundred years, but a millennium of distrust and resentment was created.

What could cause such a crazy waste of life, money and time? Two things. The first is that the rumours of the savagery of the Muslims and Jews who lived in Palestine were exaggerated by those who had much to gain from their overthrow. The second was the personal angle: according to the Popes of the time, if you were killed on a Crusade, your sins would be forgiven by God.

It's sadly ironic that the demonisation of a culture, and the prospect of immortality if you die doing the will of your God, should cause destructive wars between Muslims and the West.

Having a Big Hairy Audacious Goal is all very well, but every struggle has a cost. Someone with commitment will still count that cost, whereas a fanatic forgets it.

HERE'S AN IDEA FOR YOU...

It's easy to spoil the lives of the people around you by dragging them along in a madcap scheme. You're unlikely to lead them in a destructive war, but take a fresh look at the cost to others of your grand projects. Some victories have an unacceptably high human cost.

37 BE CAREFUL WHAT YOU WISH FOR

Success can sometimes be as hard to cope with as failure, unless you plan for it.

One of the problems with the Crusades (which is kind of like saying, 'one of the disadvantages of being sprayed with manure') is that once everyone, after months of killing, being killed, chopping off heads, pillaging, rampaging and eating their enemies, finally made it to Palestine, they didn't quite know what to do with it.

DEFINING IDEA...

More than any other time in history, mankind faces a crossroads. One path leads to despair and utter hopelessness. The other, to total extinction. Let us pray we have the wisdom to choose correctly.

~ WOODY ALLEN

You'll have to read Mackay's book to discover the full story, but the machinations among the commanders of the troops make *The Godfather* trilogy look like an episode of *Eastenders*. 'The chiefs, though they had determined to stay at Antioch for two months, could not remain quiet for so long a time. They would, in all probability, have fallen upon each other, had there been no Turks in Palestine upon whom they might vent their impetuosity,' Mackay says of the competing leaders. Several of the nobles who set off for the Crusades got there, spent some time fighting, spent more time arguing, thought 'sod this', and went home again.

The problem with launching a big project that quickly unites a disparate bunch of people is that if you actually achieve what you set out to do, you then have to deal with your success. In business terms this is a well-known problem with the takeover, especially an unwanted takeover. Everyone fights hard, wins the battle and has little or no idea what to do next, or has thought through a plan for the war, but not for the peace. The moment that the peace is declared is far too late to start the planning.

Roughly two-thirds of corporate mergers never realise their aims. That's a pretty dramatic failure rate. McKinsey, for example, did an analysis to show that many businesses when they are pressed together focus exclusively on cutting costs – that is, fixing the perceived problem. They neglect sales and innovation – in other words, what made the business worth merging with in the first place. They are so busy fighting, they don't know when to stop.

Excitement, momentum and a stop-at-nothing attitude are considered advantages in the world of business (just as they were for the Crusades), especially when you have your own city to capture. Dealmakers aren't known for being the type of people to obsessively say, 'have we thought everything through?', but, as Professor Harbir Singh at Wharton School of Management says, one of the worst things that you, as a business leader, can do is to 'fall in love' with a deal. It means you will obsessively drive yourself to its conclusion, whether or not when you get there you're better off than when you started.

HERE'S AN IDEA FOR YOU...

We make contingency plans for when we lose, but do you have one for when you win? Look beyond immediate goals and make detailed plans for success.

38 KIDS DO THE FUNNIEST THINGS

Boys will be boys. Well, not strictly. The history of the Children's Crusade is dramatic, amazing – and not really true.

DEFINING IDEA...

Youth is a wonderful thing. What a crime to waste it on children.

~ GEORGE BERNARD SHAW

In the long and bloody history of the Crusades, one of the most dramatic events was the Children's Crusade of 1212 – or, as Mackay dates it, 1213. He recounts that 30,000 children set out for the Holy Land on the advice of some monks, who led them down to the Mediterranean. 'They were, no doubt, composed of the idle and deserted children who generally swarm in great cities,' he writes, 'ready for anything.'

Whether they were ready to be sold into slave ships and transported to Africa, which is how this story ends, isn't recorded. But that's not the deal they were sold. Meanwhile Pope Innocent III, hearing how the children had bravely sacrificed themselves, hoping only to bring Christianity to Palestine, was moved to exclaim, 'These children are awake, while we sleep!', and so launched another expedition of blood-letting using adults with horses and swords.

It's a great story, but about 20% true. More recent sources have pointed out that the Latin in which the first accounts were written uses 'puer' (boy) but probably meant something more like 'young country people'. Also, there wasn't one contemporary event that matches the description of the Crusade that was given by later storytellers. The best bet is that it's a conflation of two events, where young preachers gathered crowds in France and Germany. In the first, a shepherd from Germany rounded up about 7000 youngish poor people on an expedition to the Holy Land, and got as far as Genoa, where the waters of the Mediterranean didn't part as expected. Some made their way to Palestine by other means, some tried to get across the sea and ended up sunk in a storm or maybe sold into slavery, but that was the end of that. Meanwhile another shepherd called Stephen of Cloyes claimed divine powers and seems to have led about 30,000 people down to Saint-Denis where he performed miracles. Then everyone went home.

Not such great stories, then, but the myth of the poor innocents whose piety exceeds that of other people was used to motivate unwilling would-be crusaders from relatively soon afterwards.

We still use (and abuse) the ardency and drive of children 800 years later. They are common targets for recruiters of every religion and belief. In his book *The Islamist*, Ed Husain talks about how as a naive schoolboy he and his friends were radicalised by Islamic fundamentalists and convinced to reject non-Muslims. The Communists and the Fascists knew that to have organisations of young pioneers was both a great way to recruit, and a way to shame the older generation into following along.

On the other hand, that drive can be harnessed for more positive benefits. Look at the average age of the people who are attempting to 'Make Poverty History', or volunteering in the developing world. They really are awake, when we sleep.

HERE'S AN IDEA FOR YOU...

You might not be a kid any more, but you've got skills that can complement their energy. Volunteers need organisation, experience and contacts, which come with age.

39 WHAT GOES ON TOUR

The First Crusade taught us a lesson. Shame we didn't take enough notice of it.

DEFINING IDEA...

All truths are easy to understand once they are discovered; the point is to discover them.

~ GALILEO

Crowd madnesses aren't generally positive, but they're not always a total waste of time. While it's hard to make a case that the First Crusade was a Good Thing – especially for the people who had bits of them cut off and their corpses hung from the ramparts of the castles of the Levant –

Mackay does point out that after the crusaders returned, Europe did begin to experience a large amount of beneficial social change, leading to better systems of governance and a decline in the idea that peasants were little more than cattle.

'Such pilgrims,' he says, 'as returned from the Holy Land came back with minds more liberal and expanded than when they set out. They had come in contact with a people more civilised than themselves… and had lost some portion, however small, of the prejudice and bigotry of ignorance.'

Often, after some hysterical period calms down, we take a look around, and ask, 'what were we doing?' The temptation at this moment is to turn away and learn nothing. Much better to try to learn everything you can, no matter what the cost in embarrassment and humiliation.

A model for learning is South Africa's 'Truth and Reconciliation Commission' that met during the post-apartheid era. The purpose of the Commission was to expose the stories of the madness that was apartheid, from all sides, and to avoid 'victor's justice' – which, while giving comfort to those who were injured by apartheid, would damage the chances of South Africa ever becoming a 'normal' society. While open to criticism, the Commission was undoubtedly a brave and difficult step.

Contrast this with the behaviour of many businesses or social groups when a long-term problem unravels. Often our first reaction is to cover up, to remove ourselves from any blame, and so we gloss over the stories that can help those who come after us. If the crusaders had said 'what goes on tour stays on tour', and hadn't introduced any new thinking to Europe afterwards, social change might have been delayed.

But let's not imagine that experience is a strong teacher unless it is carefully nurtured. Europe continued to be a rubbish place to be poor in for hundreds of years, religious prejudice has never gone away and Palestine is still being fought over. The population of Europe was so profoundly affected by the civilising force of the First Crusade that it, er, only launched another eight of them – though, to be fair, they simply couldn't match number one for intolerance and slaughter.

HERE'S AN IDEA FOR YOU...

Set up systems to learn from your biggest mistakes, and record your findings. It's amazing that when staff move on, their replacements can launch exactly the same hare-brained schemes without a second thought.

40 DON'T PANIC

Panics are often about more than just the thing you're panicking about.

In the fifteenth century the witch mania began to take hold. One of the reasons for the mass panic was the fear that the Antichrist was coming. The world was descending into godless chaos.

DEFINING IDEA...

I've developed a new philosophy.
I only dread one day at a time.

~ CHARLIE BROWN
(WELL, CHARLES M. SCHULTZ, HIS CREATOR)

'The more they burned, the more they found to burn,' says Mackay, pointing out that this was less about witches and external devils than the problems in people's own minds. So, while the widespread evidence of witches was seen as evidence that the Devil was alive on earth, it was more accurate to say that the panic over witches arose because people were scared of the Devil. When anything scary happened, they attributed it to the Devil, rather than to the work of ordinary humans or of nature.

So it was with the oddest mass panic of the twentieth century, which occurred in the United States on 30 October 1938. That night the young actor Orson Welles narrated his adaptation of *The War of the Worlds*, the H. G. Wells novel in which monsters arrive from Mars and invade Earth. He cleverly wrote the adaptation to sound like a real news broadcast which was reporting an invasion from Mars, and was mostly worried that people would think it was stupid: 'It was our thought that perhaps people might be bored or annoyed at hearing a tale so improbable,' he said afterwards.

The opposite occurred. When a newscaster cut into a fake dance band concert with news that he was watching an alien crawl out of a spacecraft, listeners began to panic. 'Good heavens – something's wriggling out of the shadow,' the announcer said. 'It glistens like wet leather. But that face – it … it is indescribable.' Next day the *New York Times* reported how citizens fled their houses with wet towels on their faces to protect them from Martian gas. For a week the hysteria was national news.

Like many mass panics, this was, at best, only partly true. Historians point out that the newspapers exaggerated the panic to show how irresponsible the rival radio networks were. The best estimate was that 20% of the audience was fooled. But that's still quite a chunk. Why? One of the factors was that at the time Americans were on edge as the world was about to descend into war. The broadcast cleverly aped the feel of a rocket attack which many believed might come from Germany at any time.

Mass panics don't appear out of nowhere. They piggyback on our existing worries, even the hidden ones.

HERE'S AN IDEA FOR YOU...

Don't panic more than you have to. Decide measurable standards for what events are a concern, a worry and a big problem, and what you'll do when they happen. If the value of your pension drops in a stock-market dip, for example, the best advice is often to do nothing, wait for a recovery and look at the returns over years rather than days.

41 A WITCH (ALLEGEDLY)

The witch-finder general was a dangerous man. He knew that an accusation is often enough to convict.

Matthew Hopkins – 'this vulgar man' – was, in the middle of the seventeenth century, the Witch-Finder General in Essex, which seemed to involve a lot of hard work. When he got to work in 1644, it seems Essex had a remarkable number of witches.

Stop sniggering at the back.

He was a sort of witch-ambulance-chaser. Someone suspected a witch, and bang, there he was, ready to claim his fee of twenty shillings plus travel and expenses for discovering her. In one year 'he brought sixty poor creatures to the stake'; his common test was the scarcely believable one of 'swimming'. The accused was bound hand and foot and tossed in the water. If she sank she was innocent, though somewhat dead. If she floated she was obviously a witch and would be burned.

Another test was to keep the accused in a room for 24 hours, under strict guard. She would, he said, be attended by one of her imps, who might be a fly. So if a fly came into the room and the guards were unable to catch it, she was obviously a witch. Making a mistake when reciting the Lord's Prayer was also considered proof of witchiness – even though, under the pressure that most of the accused must have felt, it would have been almost impossible to pass the test.

From this it's not hard to work out that the best way to stay alive was not to be accused, because as soon as the question was asked you were unlikely to survive. Nor were you likely to get much help from family and friends: the accused were often disowned, because the best way to be accused of witchcraft would be to stick up for someone who had just been condemned after one of the witch-finder's tests.

We no longer throw people we don't like into lakes. That doesn't mean that guilt by accusation no longer exists. In fact, it has had something of a revival in the last few years. In the hunt for Madeleine McCann, the ordeal of local resident Robert Murat is a modern equivalent: the witch-finders of the news media, once he was accused, simply decided he was guilty and tried to collect (fictitious) evidence to support the idea. Whether you like the royal family or not, the idea that they plotted to murder Princess Diana is still widely believed. It's a plot that would have failed if she had worn a seat belt, but the accusation's potency trumps common sense.

HERE'S AN IDEA FOR YOU...

Take former newspaper editor Andrew Marr's advice: if a witch-finding newspaper headline asks you a question ('Is this the most dangerous man in Britain?'), try saying 'no' in your head – and the impact disappears.

42 THE HIDDEN HAND

Conspiracy theories are often the weapon of the rich and powerful.

Nowadays we mostly know of the Knights Templar because they were involved in that thing where Jesus married Mary Magdalene and moved to France with the Holy Grail. Alternatively we know of them because they inspire an excellent fancy dress costume.

DEFINING IDEA...

The central belief of every moron is that he is the victim of a mysterious conspiracy against his common rights and true deserts.

~ H. L. MENCKEN

It's less well-known that the Knights Templar were briefly public enemy number one, accused (and convicted) of plotting with the Devil, worshipping a cat and eating babies. 'Their wealth, their power, their pride and their insolence had raised up enemies on either side,' Mackay tells us. 'Every sort of accusation was made against them, but failed to work their overthrow, until the terrible cry of witchcraft was let loose upon them.'

It's good to have someone to blame. It makes us feel comfortable and even reassured. At times of stress, when bad things which we can't explain happen to us, we often divine a hidden hand, organising things behind the scenes.

And so it was with the Templars. Set up during the Crusades, they had been extremely powerful and successful for many years. Their organisation spanned Europe and they were politically influential in just as many places. Many disliked their power and influence. When King Philip IV of France, who owed them a lot of money, hit on the idea that they might have formed a conspiracy with the Devil – and got the help of Pope Clement V to take action in 1307 – hundreds were captured, tortured, tried and burned at the stake. At one point, fifty-nine were burned in one big bonfire in Paris.

So the conspiracy was exposed. Not only were we saved from the Devil, but lots of people like Philip IV were rewarded for their torturing and burning by confiscating and sharing the Templars' possessions. The public were convinced that these murdering thieves had acted in their interests.

Conspiracy theories are often presented today as a way for ordinary people, like you and me, to divine a truth about the world that the powerful keep hidden. But that's not necessarily the case: in history, especially recent history, they have been used by the rich and powerful regularly to undermine any opposition. Stalin and Hitler both alleged conspiracies by their opponents.

There are conspiracies in the world, but what matters is that we resist any temptation to 'join the dots' when there is an easier, simpler and more likely explanation. When we succumb to conspiracy theories, we might think we are being fearlessly countercultural – but in reality we're more often serving the interests of the Philip IVs of the world.

HERE'S AN IDEA FOR YOU...

Encourage those who work for you to vent their frustration when bad things happen. Often you'll find that they've constructed a complex and fanciful narrative of what's 'really' going on, one probably dreamed up by a troublemaker with a plausible manner and much to gain. Unless you listen, you'll never know.

43 FROM THE TOP

The witch mania is a lesson in how we tend to respond to the horror of the unknown.

DEFINING IDEA...

'I must do something'
solves more problems than
'something must be done'.

~ ANON

The staggering, amazing story of the witch mania is a must-read for anyone who thinks that humans are rational creatures. This wasn't a five-week fad, or the work of one man, or a response to a single stimulus. The witch mania, as Mackay tells us, lasted for 250 years and consumed thousands of innocent people. That is, unless you think there really are witches who should be burned at the stake, in which case skip the rest of this book and read something with more pictures and short words.

The origin of the witch mania was the simple superstition that everything that went wrong was attributable to some external force: 'If a storm arose and blew down his barn, it was witchcraft... if disease fastened upon his limbs... they were not visitations of Providence, but the works of some neighbouring hag.'

We all like to blame someone or something else when something goes wrong. It's terrifying to know that bad things happen to people who don't deserve it. It's even more terrifying to know that we tend to look for someone to blame who has absolutely nothing to do with it.

This is top-down thinking, and we are all susceptible to it. It's one of the ways in which the popular press can hoodwink us, by finding some umbrella term – illegal immigrants, benefit cheats, fat-cat bosses – and selling us stories that fit our preconceptions.

The individual stories may be correct. For example, there were plenty of city traders who took home a lot of cash that, with hindsight, they didn't deserve (by the middle of 2008, London's traders had taken home £12.6 billion in bonuses for that year alone). That does not mean that anyone who works in business and who earns more than you or me does not deserve their money.

There are many people who cheat their benefits. The government calculates the cost at £800 million. That doesn't make everyone who claims benefits a cheat.

Top-down thinking can be a relief – it means that if we categorise things simply (note that newspapers consider that everything either makes you fat or makes you thin, gives you cancer or cures it), it gives us a simple pre-determined set of enemies, and means that we don't have to take responsibility. One of the biggest determinants of whether we will be overweight or get cancer is our lifestyle – but while there are external factors we can blame instead, it's best not to think about that. Personally, I blame the fat cats.

HERE'S AN IDEA FOR YOU...

It's easy to decide that you like or don't like someone instantly and never revisit that decision, even though it says more about you than it does about them. Take another look. You might be missing out on good friends, interesting colleagues and talented employees.

44 THE DEAD PUPPY STATUTE

There's not a lot we can admire about those who propagated the witch mania. But we have to admit that they were adept at the art of counting and naming demons.

DEFINING IDEA...

It's all a matter of marketing.

~ JAMES L. MARTIN

If you believe in real, physical demons these days, people tend to put you in the funny farm. Unlike in the Middle Ages, where, as Mackay relates, St Gregory of Nice could tell the story of a nun who forgot to say 'benedicte' before sitting down to dinner, and accidentally swallowed a demon that was hiding under a lettuce leaf. Don't tell this to your kids. It's hard enough to get them to eat lettuce as it is.

One of the ways that the misguidedly pious in those days could frighten the wits out of the common people was to be nuttily precise about how many demons there were, what they did and even what their names were. An expert called Wierus counted them: 7,405,926, divided into seventy-two battalions. It would take quite a large salad to hide all of them at once.

The rituals by which the demons could be summoned were recounted in bizarre detail. Satan usually appeared as a goose, a duck, a goat, a cat or any number of other common animals. It helped to keep people on their guard. Was that a man walking along with his goat, or was it a satanic ritual? It's the equivalent nowadays of saying the devil takes the form of an iPod or a mobile phone (which, of course, it's quite possible to believe).

All of this seems positively sane compared to the wonderful barminess of the names that the accusers gave to the demons that witches are supposed to have conjured. Seeing as the witches protested innocence, and were usually just some crazy old people whose crimes were often being ugly, weird or just unpopular (and also because demons don't exist), they were unlikely to have come up with the names themselves, so we have to credit their persecutors instead. One Mother Samuel, accused of being a witch, evidently had personal demons known as First Smack, Second Smack, Third Smack, Catch, Hardname and Blue. Even better, another accuser named imps called the Roaring Lion, Wait-Upon-Herself and Ranting Roarer, and claimed that the Devil had rebaptised his witches with names like Pickle-nearest-the-wind and Over-the-dike-with-it.

No, I don't either.

Why does this interest us? Because it's in the finest tradition of giving a dog a bad name, which we often meet in the witch-like field of tax politics. We don't recall the Community Charge with much emotion, but we hated the Poll Tax. Inheritance Tax isn't very newsworthy, but when James L. Martin, president of the Sixty Plus Association in the US, renamed it the 'Death Tax' in a press conference, he uncovered a whole new layer of outrage.

HERE'S AN IDEA FOR YOU...

Thinking up snappy insulting names for things you don't like isn't easy, but it's fun and it makes them stick in people's memory. No one cares about by-law 17.1 section 2, paragraph 4, but call it the Dead Puppy Statute, and sane people will chain themselves to railings about it.

45 SLOW POISON

It's hard to describe slow poisoning as a popular delusion or a crowd madness. But it was relatively popular in the past, as in some quarters it wasn't considered nearly as bad as quick poisoning. Crazy, yes: but does it still exist?

DEFINING IDEA...

A great many people think they are thinking when they are merely rearranging their prejudices.

~ WILLIAM JAMES

Mackay's chapter on slow poison makes odd reading: the idea that in the seventeenth century it 'spread over Europe like a pestilence' is certainly Mackay's journalistic impulse getting the better of him. It was hardly a crowd madness in the same league as the witch mania or the Crusades.

But it did claim its victims, and the perpetrators often profited from the odd idea that to wrong someone gradually, by degrees, was not nearly as bad as doing them a quick, bumper-sized wrong. Mackay says this was worst in Italy: 'From a very early period, it seems to have been looked on in that country as a perfectly justifiable means of getting rid of an enemy,' he says. In the reign of Pope Alexander VII (a time when the Popes themselves weren't above a bit of skulduggery if it suited them), 'young widows were unusually abundant' in Rome. Priests were reporting that a lot of them had confessed that they had done away with their husbands by poison. The source was a society of young wives who got their poison from a 'hag' called Hieronyma Spira.

We live in an age where La Spira and her black widows would find it harder to succeed, but it doesn't mean that some sections of society aren't metaphorically getting away with murder. One form of (usually) non-fatal poison which future societies will look back on as proof that we weren't as modern as we thought is institutionalised prejudice.

Many years ago, I interviewed Lord Browne when he was the CEO of BP. We now know that he is gay, which maybe was why he was so committed to giving everyone in his industry a fair chance to succeed. To do that he had his interview panels audited in case they were unconsciously racist or sexist; he hated the idea that the world's most talented people were all born white and male and went to a handful of universities, and was actively trying to dismantle it, he told me.

The problem in identifying a slow poison like institutional prejudice is that it's almost impossible to spot at any moment. The pattern that certain people don't get the job because they're not one of us, that they get treated slightly worse because of their colour or religion rather than their ability, results in a slow drip-drip of failure that often reinforces that prejudice: we gave them a chance, but they're not up to it.

Companies love the idea of diversity but few pay more than lip service to the ideal. Slow poison today doesn't kill rich husbands, but arguably it's more dangerous to society than ever.

HERE'S AN IDEA FOR YOU...

Create a diversity policy – but it needs measurable goals, and someone external to audit it, or it's just a good intention. There are consultancies that will do this for you.

46 SIMPLEST IS BEST

Occam's razor stops us believing barmy things.

The belief in the hundreds of haunted houses in Europe, Mackay tells us, is reminiscent of the witch mania in its silliness, but is 'comparatively harmless'.

DEFINING IDEA...

Plurality should not be posited without necessity.
~ WILLIAM OF OCCAM

It doesn't mean that it hasn't been a good earner for the unscrupulous, though. For example, take the excellent story of the thirteenth-century monks of St Bruno, who wanted to establish an order near Paris. Having identified the palace of Vauvert near their smaller dwelling that would be very suitable, 'somehow or other it almost immediately afterwards began to acquire a bad name,' as Mackay says.

The king, disturbed that there were spirits walking around one of his palaces, was told that – if they could move in – the poor monks would do everything they could to banish the ghosts. Funnily enough, when he signed the palace over to them, the hauntings suddenly stopped.

Today few of us would sign over an entire building based on a few unusual sightings, but relatively sane people will decide on bizarre chains of cause and effect based on their prejudices and fears. An example: a large part of the population, including some quite clever people, has decided that the pregnant Princess Diana was murdered by the secret services working for Prince Philip so that a Muslim would not inherit the throne. If you heard it for the first time today, you'd burst out laughing, but bit by bit it has seeped into our consciousness.

How do we guard against wasting our time, looking silly or being afraid of ghosts that don't exist? Use the principle of Occam's razor, attributed to William of Occam, who lived in the fourteenth century. It states that any explanation of any phenomenon should make as few assumptions as possible. The simplest solution is usually the best.

So, for example, a murder plot that would involve the participation of the police in two countries, an ambulance crew, ministers in two governments and an entire royal family, which would not have achieved its stated aim (the then-divorced Princess Diana would not have given birth to the heir to any throne) and which would have been thwarted had she worn a seat belt, is a pretty complicated explanation for a tragic car accident.

That's not to say that the complicated explanation is never true. For example, maybe unquiet spirits from another plane of existence did haunt the palace of Vauvert and the monks really were selflessly helping the king...

Mackay thought that ghosts were ludicrous in 1842, but we see them just as often now as our ancestors did then.

HERE'S AN IDEA FOR YOU...

Occam's razor isn't foolproof, but it's practical. For example, if you're not making sales, it might be because the customer went to school with your competitor and they are both Sunderland fans. Or it might be that your product isn't as good. The complicated explanation might be true but offers no hope; the simple, rational one suggests something you can improve.

47 WE FOUND THAT FUNNY?

Short-lived crazes irritate us, but these days they sell an idea first.

DEFINING IDEA...

Imitation is at least 50% of the creative process.

~ JAMIE BUCKINGHAM,
RELIGIOUS WRITER

One of the fashions of Victorian London that you might have missed was the short-lived craze for exclaiming 'Quoz!' Kids would shout it at surprised passers-by; someone asked a favour who didn't want to perform it would use it as an explanation. It became, Mackay reminds his readers (and reveals to us) the sort of phrase you heard everywhere.

Which goes to show that the fashion for Internet 'virals' isn't about the Internet. It's about our desire to share something which, for a short time, we all find entertaining. For example, remember the craze in 1999 for shouting 'whassup!' at your friends when you met them, or called them on the phone? It lasted for several years, based on the Budweiser advertisement of the time. Dance songs that included 'Whazzup' by True Party in 2000 (it reached thirteen on the UK Singles Chart – if you bought it, you should be thoroughly ashamed of yourself) drilled the phrase into our heads, for a short time. And then we woke up. By 2002 it was being ridiculed in *The Simpsons* (always a good marker of when to give up on something).

And of course, there's Crazy Frog – or, as it was originally and more accurately known, 'annoying thing'. Based on a recording of a seventeen-year-old student impersonating a two-stroke engine, the sound became an animation, a ringtone that made £14 million through downloads in the UK alone and a novelty recording act.

How does this sort of thing catch on? These virals need to be in some way amusing (so they get passed on), entertaining, and easy to understand and copy. Viral campaigns are now an object of legitimate study, and one of the conclusions of this research is that they are spread by alpha users – people who are well-connected and influential. If a music hall star in Mackay's time started saying 'Quoz!' in their act, then it would catch on. Today, identifying and reaching those alpha users is a service that many marketers pay big money for.

Why? One difference between the virals of Mackay's era and ours is that often ours have a profit motive attached: virals advertise a product, or are themselves a way to make a profit. Using the irritating Frog as an example, the company that licensed the sound as a ringtone bought 73,716 advertising spots on British TV in May 2005 alone. One in ten Brits saw the advert sixty times. Arguably, that's more of a sledgehammer than a virus.

Getting your message out virally can be incredibly effective. It doesn't have to mean advertising a service on the Internet or selling a ringtone – we do the same thing when we try and build enthusiasm behind a charity day at work. Try something, but not the Crazy Frog. Please.

HERE'S AN IDEA FOR YOU...

You want to get a message out to your community? Identify the best-connected people who people take notice of – remember, it's not usually the boss – to be your alpha users. But unless the message amuses or entertains them, it won't be passed on.

48 CHATTIN BREEZE

When people around you say things you don't understand, that's the way language has always been.

DEFINING IDEA...

Incomprehensible jargon is the hallmark of a profession.

~ KINGMAN BREWSTER, JR.
FORMER PRESIDENT OF YALE

In listing the preposterous phrases of the time, even Mackay struggles to work out exactly why they came into use, and what they represent. It's not surprising.

For six months, we learn, people walked around singing 'The sea, the sea', for no particular reason. Phrases like 'Does your mother know you're out?' and 'There he goes with his eye out' vied for popularity with 'What a shocking bad hat' and 'Has your mother sold her mangle?' The last one, Mackay points out, didn't achieve the same popularity as many of the others because it was hard to apply in many situations. Try it in the pub tonight. It's really very tricky.

The meaninglessness of these phrases meant that when they were lost to the language no one really regretted it. But Mackay defends them as 'whimseys', and for those who objected to meaningless new phrases popping up, he points out that a wise man would say 'if they cannot be happy, at least let them be merry'.

Many of us are not nearly as tolerant today of the modern affectations of language, of which there are many. Indeed, recently Parentline Plus set up www.gotateenager.org.uk to explain to confused parents what their kids were actually saying when they told their parents they were 'chattin breeze' (talking rubbish).

When you're confronted in emails by text message abbreviations, slang, colloquialisms and hip phrases that you don't get, it's tempting to say 'this isn't English'. You're right, up to a point. It's not the language that you recognise, but it is English – a language that has always evolved. What for you is indecipherable rubbish is perfectly plain to many of the people around you (especially if they are younger than you, or just more open-minded).

At work it's frustrating when you hear the people who work for you talking, or see them emailing, and using words and phrases that you consider have no meaning. But if you seek to impose a standard language on all the communication at work, as many bosses try to do, be careful what you're approving.

If you are intolerant of contemporary slang but approve of equally baffling office jargon like 'low-hanging fruit' or 'thinking outside the box', you're no different to them. You just happen to inhabit the adminisphere, and they're in the cube farm. There's probably one other way you are different. You're older.

HERE'S AN IDEA FOR YOU...

If you're frustrated by the written English in your company's internal systems, it's not always the solution to impose a single vocabulary. What matters is that each party can understand what's being said. Make rules for external communication, then have a war on all jargon. But face it – English is changing. It's not Latin.

49 ORDINARY DECENT CRIMINALS

We find organised crime exciting, thrilling and entertaining. Why?

The French traveller Abbé de Blanc wrote home in the 1750s, Mackay tells us at the beginning of his chapter which expresses open wonderment at why we seem to admire great thieves, that 'he continually met with Englishmen who were not less vain in boasting of the success of their highwaymen than the bravery of their troops'. They may be thieves, we say, but they are our thieves.

It's a long tradition to imagine that career criminals are somehow thrilling. 'There is a heroism in crime as well as in virtue. Vice and infamy have their altars and their religion,' wrote William Hazlitt, in Mackay's era – a man who obviously hadn't much experience of crack dealers or car thieves.

DEFINING IDEA...

No great scoundrel is ever uninteresting.

~ MURRAY KEMPTON, JOURNALIST AND CIVIL RIGHTS ACTIVIST

Today we're just as bad, if not worse. What's your favourite film? Maybe it's *The Godfather*. Or *Goodfellas*. The best television show of the last ten years? A lot of us would say that it's *The Sopranos*. We're transfixed by the romance of major thieves who live without compromise, who impose their own moral code and who get to enjoy the power and influence that we only dream of.

It was the same in Mackay's time, when the romantic criminals were those of the previous century, highwaymen like Dick Turpin or the prison-breaker Jack Sheppard. In London's East End you can still hear some of the older generation tell you of the Kray twins, and how you were safe on the streets when they were in charge.

This popular delusion, and the way in which we are willing to believe it, is exploited by organised crime groups today. In many countries in the world, they control a lot of front companies which exist as little more than ways to launder their cash, and in many communities they are protected.

Bernardo Provenzano, who took over the running of the Cosa Nostra in Italy in the 1990s, rebuilt it by specifically tapping into public goodwill. He cut down on the executions, and told his local bosses to concentrate on providing services for the people and co-operating with public institutions. Why? Because if they did this, he argued, organised crime would be relatively unimpeded in its basic job of fleecing people for cash. If you find this admirable or amusing, then don't bother complaining next time you hear about corruption or inefficiency in public services.

Provenzano's dedication to the cause of inspiring admiration from the public, while not killing people in quite so obvious a way, earned him the nickname of 'the Accountant'. All very admirable. But if you want a more apposite description as to what really goes on when you deal with career criminals, his other nickname provides a clue. In Sicilian, he was known as 'Binnie the tractor', because, in the words of one informant, 'he mows people down'.

HERE'S AN IDEA FOR YOU...

Criminals thrive on tolerance, especially in parts of the world in which corruption is endemic. Research shows that small levels of unchecked corruption always lead to a more serious problem, so make sure that anyone who works for you around the world knows that you have a policy of zero tolerance.

50 THEIR OWN RULES

The idea that white-collar crime is to be tolerated or even admired would have amazed Mackay. But, 150 years later, that's what we do.

DEFINING IDEA...

What I did in my youth is hundreds of times easier today. Technology breeds crime.

~ FRANK ABAGNALE, LEGENDARY CON MAN

'The populace of all countries look with admiration upon great and successful thieves,' writes Mackay. We enjoy that they dare to do what we would not dare, that they don't feel constrained by rules, and that their lives (as retold by film-makers and cheap novelists) are simply more interesting.

One of the ways in which we admire thieves today is that we distinguish them by the colour of their shirt: 'white-collar crime', as defined by the FBI, is suggested by the agency to cost the US more than $300 billion every year. The FBI has a narrow definition of white-collar crime: they define it as deceit, concealment or violation of trust without force or violence. Others define it more broadly, as any crime committed by someone with a high social status.

Whatever the definition, white-collar criminals are certainly real thieves – and, if most of the population isn't openly admiring them (unlike the mafia or highwaymen there's nothing particularly romantic about an insider trader, or someone who routinely skims money from government), very little concerted effort is made to bring them to justice compared to the perpetrators of more violent crimes.

That's partly understandable, but only partly. We struggle to find a victim for a case of money laundering, for example, or we lazily consider that 'they're all criminals' – it's just that some successful businesspeople don't break the law. We dismiss it with a shrug as just an extension of aggressive tax avoidance schemes or creative accounting. Or we even tip our hat to the corporate swindlers who use illegal schemes we barely understand to extract and hide millions.

But the bank employee who routinely hides the proceeds of violent crime is just as culpable as the criminal who robs it from a bank – without the white-collar criminal, serious blue-collar crime, especially organised crime, can't flourish.

We are biologically set up to respond to situations of danger, and to sympathise with fellow humans when they are directly threatened. White-collar crime doesn't excite us like this.

If you consider that the businesses that are robbed employ people, and pay tax, and that the support given to organised crime by white-collar criminals makes their violent and destructive crimes possible, there's nothing to admire here. Tolerating white-collar crime also perpetuates the idea (which was old-fashioned even for Mackay) that posh people make their own rules. It's pathetic.

Even on the narrowest definition, White-Collar Crime Inc. would be the world's largest company. You've already got enough competition in your business from people who don't break the law.

HERE'S AN IDEA FOR YOU...

White-collar crime thrives in organisations where there's no clear expectation of ethical behaviour, and where people are not trained how to spot it or know how to deal with it. Central to this is an anonymous whistleblowing procedure. You should have one. Whistleblowers are protected by law; train staff and managers to encourage them.

51 PISTOLS AT DAWN

Our concept of honour often leads us to self-destructive behaviour.

There's nothing worse than being insulted in public. Well, actually, being beaten up because you asked someone for a fight because they insulted you in public probably is quite a bit worse. Especially if the insult was that you were no good at fighting.

DEFINING IDEA...

I thoroughly disapprove of duels.
If a man should challenge me,
I would take him kindly and
forgivingly by the hand and lead
him to a quiet place and kill him.
~ MARK TWAIN

The curse of fighting to protect honour has changed since Mackay took a brief trot through the mad history of duelling. 'The list of duels that have sprung from the most degrading causes might be stretched out to an almost infinite extent. Sterne's father fought a duel about a goose; and the great Raleigh about a tavern-bill,' he says. Mackay also tells about a duel fought between Victorian gentlemen because one man's dog had attacked another man's dog, and of a man called Best who killed Lord Camelford ('a confirmed duellist') over an argument about the affections of a prostitute.

Of course, we don't do anything like that today. Not when you have really important things to attack other people about, such as your postcode. In London in 2007 the Metropolitan Police claimed there were 169 separate street gangs, one quarter of which had been involved in some way in a murder. The streets or parks on the boundaries between specific areas, often postcodes, had become battlegrounds.

Just as it's impossible to work out why anyone would fight a duel over a goose, it's hard to work out why a gang from London E11 would fight to protect its territory against incursions from the inhabitants of neighbouring E15. I've lived in both postcodes, and frankly they should be putting more effort into stopping people from leaving. But our tendency to look for something to defend, even at the risk of our own lives, shows how important 'identity' is to us. In the 1840s that identity was bound up with one's status as a 'gentleman'. In some of the quarrels which Mackay recounts, and which led to a fatal duel, you have to read the story twice to work out exactly whose honour had been insulted. For the gentlemen of the era, their bizarre code of honour was at times every bit as important to them as their lives – rather like the gang members of today who can be insulted by the wrong bloke walking down 'their' streets.

When we want to belong to something, the belonging is often more important than the exact thing to which we're pledging allegiance. And when we want to win a fight, the winning is often more important than whether or not we should be fighting at all.

HERE'S AN IDEA FOR YOU...

If you're planning a duel, why not try to build a bridge instead? We don't settle arguments with pistols any more, but sometimes the desire to win is only satisfied by destroying the enemy. Do that, and often you'll lose more than you gain – especially if your foe was a friend, a member of your family or your boss.

52 ESPECIALLY FOR YOU

Nowadays we still like our relics, but we prefer them to be secular.

DEFINING IDEA...

Autograph-hunting is the most unattractive manifestation of sex-starved curiosity.

~ LAURENCE OLIVIER

Religious relics aren't as popular now as they were in past times. As Mackay puts it, 'Many a nail, cut from the filthy foot of some unscrupulous ecclesiastic, was sold at a diamond's price, within six months after its severance from its parent toe, upon the supposition that it had once belonged to a saint. Peter's toes were uncommonly prolific, for there were nails enough in Europe… to have filled a sack.'

Ick.

Today religious relics are mostly a way to liven up the visit to a church on a rainy day during some European weekend break, where you can see a small silver box in a vault containing the eyelash of a saint you've never heard of. In our secular society we don't bother with this sort of thing. Or do we?

Instead, we collect memorabilia or all types of personal rubbish, which, by sticking it on the desk or wall, somehow confers an attribute on us. We don't hang an ugly signed football shirt in reception because it looks good. Instead, it says: 'I'm well connected. And successful.'

But anyone who has been present at a signing will know exactly how this is done. The shirt, ball, cricket bat or photo isn't signed with personal love and consideration – it's part of an industrial process which dumps a pile of the product in front of the celebrity, who whips out a magic marker and does whatever stylised squiggle that used to be their signature. Some even delight in the impersonal nature of this modern-day production line: in July 2008 Salman Rushdie bragged to the *Guardian* that he had signed 1000 books in 57 minutes during his latest book tour. That's one every 3.4 seconds. The literary titan whose record he beat was the wine writer Malcolm Gluck, who took 59 minutes to sign 1001. Ken Follett once signed 2050 books in 3 hours. If you have any of these books, you must be delighted that you have something so carefully dedicated to you. You might as well sign it yourself.

Fake sports memorabilia is now so widespread that the FBI has set up a specific task force dedicated to tracking it down. In the US, where signed baseball cards or basketball shorts, or little tiny American footballs, are a fixture of many offices, the counterfeit signed sports memorabilia market is worth £100 million a year. Read it again: yes, that's just the counterfeits.

This exploits our desire as fans, the idea that somehow this ownership conveys respectability on us or brings us luck – and if you don't mind the high probability that you bought a fake, go ahead and bid in that eBay auction. Future generations, we can fairly predict, will look upon these signatures with the same confusion that we look upon the veneration of the toenail or the fanatical desire to secure a rare tulip bulb.

HERE'S AN IDEA FOR YOU...

If your office is cluttered with signed pictures and sports memorabilia, get rid of it. Concentrate on your own achievements, not the achievements of people who don't care about you and probably never met you.

INDEX